ANOTHER CUP OF

sugar

ANOTHER CUP OF

sugar

ANNA OLSON

whitecap

Third printing 2007

Edited by Elaine Jones
Proofread by Elizabeth McLean
Design by Roberta Batchelor
Typeset & colours by Diane Yee
Photography by Douglas Bradshaw Photography

Printed and bound in Canada

LIBRARY AND ARCHIVES CANADA CATALOGUING IN PUBLICATION

Olson, Anna, 1968–
    Another cup of sugar / Anna Olson.

Includes index.
ISBN 1-55285-809-X
ISBN 978-1-55285-809-7

    1. Desserts. I. Title.
TX773.O458 2006   641.8'6   C2006-902339-5

The publisher acknowledges the financial support of the Government of Canada through the Book Publishing Industry Development Program for our publishing activities. We also acknowledge the financial support of the Province of British Columbia through the Book Publishing Tax Credit.

Acknowledgements

❖ ❖ ❖ This book hardly feels like work, thanks to the support and help of so many.

The cheerful personalities behind the production of Sugar for Food Network Canada are the first to thank. Without them, Sugar wouldn't be where it is today. A special word of thanks is deserved by Claudia Bianchi, whose time and talent is appreciated every day on set, but particularly valued as we created the photos for this book.

And where would I be without the sweetest person in my life, my husband Michael? He watches out for me and keeps me smiling, and no girl could ask for a kinder, more caring partner in life.

A special thank you also goes to the staff at Olson Foods + Bakery. They indulge my wacky ideas and crazy schedule and work so hard to make the business run smoothly.

And my life full of lessons could not be so rich without the unfailing love and support of my parents.

Introduction

✧ ✧ ✧ Enjoying a little something sweet is a celebration in itself. This could be as festive as a significant birthday or a weekend get-together with friends, or as simple as a quiet moment to yourself with a cookie and a cup of tea. The celebration begins not with the eating, though, but with the baking. The fact that we take time to bake is the true beginning. So what motivates us to get in the kitchen and get busy?

BAKING FOR SHARING: Our generous nature shines when baking. We bake for those we love as an expression of our affection—dessert is that little extra at the end of the meal that makes us smile. Desserts are also a big part of a special celebration. Whether it's a birthday, anniversary or wedding, a cake is usually the crowning jewel of the occasion, and there's such a sense of pride, too, as the bearer of the cake presents it to the recipient.

But baking and sweets aren't always about grand occasions and fanfare. A batch of cookies made on a rainy day or as an after-school treat can be even more memorable than a chocolate birthday cake. That little break when you indulge in a bite of brownie can lift your whole afternoon. I love the sight of a square pan of coffee cake left on the kitchen counter with a butter knife in the pan, so that anyone walking by can sneak a nibble.

A homemade dessert is always warmly received and relished, partly because the one who made it put thought, time and effort into making it.

BAKING FOR LEARNING: I don't believe people when they try to tell me, "I can cook, but I can't bake." The art of baking is not an inherited genetic trait, nor is it an intuitive skill that some have while others don't. Almost all of our time in the kitchen is spent cooking savoury things such as pasta, meats and vegetables, to feed our families. How do you know when the pasta is cooked? You know because you've made it 1,000 times before and you know how long it takes. How do you know when a cake is done? If you've only made a cake once before, it's a little more difficult to tell, but with practice, you will come to know how to read the signs.

My husband, Michael, and I have recently taken to cooking Indian cuisine, using a great Indian cookbook written by a good friend. We actually follow the recipes, since it is a style of cooking very different from our western culinary training. As we make the recipes more often, we become more comfortable with these new techniques and ingredients, and I regard learning to bake the same way. With practice you'll come to be familiar with butter and flour and sugar and eggs, and what they look like when blended and when baked.

For an even more enriching experience in the kitchen, bake with others. Just as eating a dessert is an act of sharing, so is baking with others. I especially love to see kids in the kitchen, with their friends, siblings, parents or grandparents. My grandmother was my inspiration to become a chef and my fondest memories of her are of the two of us in the kitchen—we may have been years apart in age, but in the kitchen we could speak the same language.

Baking with children allows us to take part in their fascination. It's magic to watch children develop their motor skills by stirring, beating and pouring, learn how to measure and watch with wonder as that squishy mixture they created transforms into brownies in the oven. Watching broccoli cook is not nearly so interesting (nor so delicious).

BAKING FOR SELF: By baking for self, I don't mean baking a lemon meringue pie to sit and eat with a spoon right out of the pan (though after a really tough day, it certainly can be therapeutic).

Baking for self is about the quiet pleasure of working with your hands, the sense of satisfaction that comes from creating something. You may well feel a sense of accomplishment when you make a pot of chilli on the stove, but pull a freshly made apple pie out of the oven and you want to leave it on the kitchen counter not just to cool, but to show it off! Why do you think cake stands are so popular? We want to display our cakes like trophies.

Baking for self is about satisfying our senses, as well. The aroma of baked goods in the oven warms the heart, whether it's banana bread, chocolate cookies or lemon scones. You can have that heavenly scent and something delicious to eat as well!

So draw on any motivation that works for you — sharing, learning or self. Whatever your reason or inspiration, just bake!

ANOTHER CUP OF SUGAR: This sequel to my first cookbook, *Sugar*, follows the same recipe pattern as the first book. Each section focuses on an ingredient, a key element used in baking. Within each ingredient section there is a straightforward recipe — something that doesn't take long to put together and uses ingredients you probably have in your pantry any day of the week. Then there is the "switch up," where I reconfigure that easy recipe to make it a little fancier, or add a sauce or serve it a little differently. This is to show you that there is flexibility in dessert recipes. Flavours and presentation can be easily changed, and hopefully you will recognize this as permission to play with your own recipes.

The other recipe in each section is the "showy" dessert. It may follow more classic techniques or take a little more time to make, but it will result in a masterpiece — fit for presenting at the end of a special meal. Each of these recipes includes notes and comments to guide you through — I'm there to help you, but please make sure you take full credit for your sense of satisfaction!

For fun, I thought it would be interesting in this book to arrange these ingredient themes by their colour. Making desserts inspires my sense of whimsy and hopefully yours, too. When thumbing through the book, bear in mind the original colour of those key ingredients or elements — for instance, Chocolate Applesauce Cakes may be a rich brown colour, but the key ingredient of applesauce is yellow, so you'll find the recipe is found in the chapter Yellow.

Fill your home with the wonderful aromas of baking, and enjoy the smiles that accompany the tasty results of your efforts.

"Clear" may not technically qualify as a colour, but that's not to say that an ingredient that lacks pigment must lack taste—far from it.

Often with clarity come simplicity and elegance. Our two clear ingredients, champagne and floral essences, are delicate, subtle and feminine, and the desserts made with them are light and refreshing.

clear

CHAMPAGNE | ESSENCES

Champagne

Champagne turns any occasion into a celebration, and now that decent champagne comes in smaller bottles, you don't need a crowd to indulge in a delight that needs to be consumed immediately after it's been opened.

Champagne Peach Sorbet

SERVES 6

³/₄ cup	175 mL	sugar
³/₄ cup	175 mL	water
4	4	large peaches
3 Tbsp	45 mL	fresh lemon juice
1¹/₂ cup	375 mL	chilled champagne
1	1	large egg white, lightly beaten

This sorbet has a beautiful rosy blush to it, just like my cheeks after a glass of bubbly.

❖ ❖ ❖

Bring sugar and water to a boil, stirring to dissolve sugar, remove from heat and allow to cool completely. To peel peaches, immerse in boiling water for 1 minute, then remove and cool before slipping off skins. Slice peaches and place in food processor or blender with cooled sugar syrup. Blend until liquefied. Strain liquid and stir in lemon juice.

Immediately before adding to ice cream maker, stir in chilled champagne and egg white. Freeze following manufacturer's instructions. Spoon sorbet into a non-reactive container and freeze for at least 4 hours before serving.

NOTES

❖ If your peaches are quite firm, the trick of peeling by blanching them in boiling water won't always work. In that case, I just use a sharp vegetable peeler.

❖ Champagne refers to the sparkling wine from the Champagne region of France. In this recipe, a bottle of Prosecco, Italy's sweet sparkling wine, works just fine.

❖ The egg white holds air in the sorbet, so that it is smooth-tasting and easy to scoop. It can be omitted, if you wish.

Peach Bellini Floats

1 ½ cups	375 mL	peach nectar
1 bottle	750 mL	rosé champagne or Prosecco wine
		slices of fresh peach, for garnish

A Bellini is an elegant champagne cocktail accented with peach nectar. This frosty version is even fancier, perfect to toast a grand announcement.

❖ ❖ ❖

For each bellini float, pour 2 Tbsp (30 mL) of peach nectar into the bottom of a champagne flute (use a spoon to pour the nectar in so it goes right to the bottom). Spoon two small scoops of Champagne Peach Sorbet into the flutes and slowly pour in the wine. Garnish with a slice of fresh peach and serve.

Champagne Fruit Jellies

Champagne Fruit Jellies

1 1/2 cups	375 mL	fresh raspberries
1 cup	250 mL	sliced strawberries
1 cup	250 mL	fresh blackberries
1 1/2 cups	375 mL	water
1 1/2 cups	375 mL	sugar
1	1	peach, sliced (skin on)
1 strip	1 strip	lemon peel (yellow part only)
3 cups	750 mL	chilled Champagne or sparkling wine
3 Tbsp	45 mL	gelatin powder
		fresh peach slices and mint, for garnish

These jellies, served in champagne flutes, make a darling finish to Sunday brunch or a patio supper.

✧ ✧ ✧

Arrange raspberries, strawberries and blackberries in 8 champagne flutes and chill. Bring water and sugar up to a simmer. Once sugar has dissolved, add sliced peach and lemon peel and simmer for 3 minutes. Remove peach, cool slightly and peel off skin if it comes off easily (otherwise peel with a paring knife). Place a slice in each flute. Pour 1/2 cup (125 mL) of wine over gelatin to soften for a minute. Stir softened gelatin into warm sugar syrup and return to heat to dissolve. Allow to cool to room temperature. Stir in remaining wine. While still bubbly, ladle wine mixture slowly over fruit, until the top of fruit is just covered. Chill flutes until jelly is almost set, then top with remaining wine mixture. Chill for at least 3 hours before serving.

Garnish each flute with a slice of peach and a sprig of mint.

NOTES

✧ It is important to thoroughly chill champagne before opening. An unchilled bottle is more likely to pop and bubble over when opened, and you don't want to lose one precious drop (unless you're christening a boat or celebrating your Stanley Cup victory).

✧ I find it helpful to chill the champagne flutes with the fruit while preparing the jelly. This helps accelerate the setting of the jelly, to keep as many lovely champagne bubbles as possible within the jelly.

✧ This recipe can also be made in a 9- × 5-inch (2-L) loaf pan lined with plastic wrap. I layer the fruit in the pan and carefully ladle the jelly liquid in. After setting, I unmould it and slice it to show off the beautifully suspended fruits.

Essences

By essences, I mean the subtle fragrance and aromas that flower waters can lend to dessert. Rosewater is the most common and is typical in Middle Eastern desserts, such as Turkish Delight. It is relatively easy to find at specialty markets and health food stores.

Rosewater Rice Pudding

This rice pudding is a light and refreshing dessert, different from a typically thick, custard-style rice pudding. It's perfect after a spicy Thai or Indian supper.

✧ ✧ ✧

RICE PUDDING

1 1/2 cups	375 mL	whole milk
1	1	14-oz (300-mL) tin coconut milk
3/4 cup	175 mL	jasmine or basmati rice
1 cup	250 mL	sugar
6	6	whole green cardamom pods
2	2	cinnamon sticks
1 Tbsp	15 mL	rosewater

FOR PUDDING, bring milk, coconut milk, rice and sugar to a simmer. Lightly crush cardamom pods with a knife and add to rice with cinnamon sticks. Simmer uncovered, stirring often, until reduced by half, about 40 minutes. Remove cardamom and cinnamon. Stir in rosewater and chill.

TOPPING

2 Tbsp	30 mL	water
2 Tbsp	30 mL	sugar
2 cups	500 mL	sliced strawberries
1/2 cup	125 mL	shelled pistachios, roughly chopped
1 tsp	5 mL	rosewater
1/2 tsp	2 mL	ground pink peppercorns

FOR TOPPING, heat water and sugar to dissolve. Allow to cool. Toss strawberries and pistachios in syrup and stir in rosewater and pink peppercorns. Spoon topping over each serving of rice pudding.

NOTES

✧ This rice pudding is all about the fragrance. So many elements contribute to its subtle aroma—the basmati or jasmine rice, the coconut milk, the cardamom and cinnamon, and of course, the rosewater.

✧ If you'd like to make this dessert, but would rather skip (or can't locate) rosewater, consider using a vanilla bean or 2 jasmine green tea bags as alternative fragrances.

✧ Note that I like to use cinnamon stick, not ground cinnamon—it adds fragrance and taste without colouring the pudding at all.

Coconut Rice Truffles

1 1/3 cups	325 mL	sweetened coconut

DIPPING SAUCE

2 cups	500 mL	sliced strawberries
2 Tbsp	30 mL	water
2 Tbsp	30 mL	sugar
1 tsp	5 mL	rose water
1/2 tsp	2 mL	ground pink peppercorns

Cool, chilled rice pudding shaped into truffles makes excellent dessert "hors d'oeuvres."

✧ ✧ ✧

Prepare and chill Rosewater Rice Pudding (page 17). For truffles, dip hands in cool water and shape small spoonfuls of pudding. Roll truffles in coconut and chill until ready to serve.

FOR DIPPING SAUCE, purée strawberries with water, sugar, rosewater and pink peppercorns. Strain and chill until ready to serve. Alternatively, make a strawberry salad by leaving strawberries in slices and tossing with water, sugar, rosewater and pink peppercorns. Serve truffles with dipping sauce or strawberry salad.

Flower Party Cookies

COOKIES

1 ¼ cups	300 mL	unsalted butter, room temperature
1 cup	250 mL	sugar
1	1	large egg
1 tsp	5 mL	vanilla extract
2 tsp	10 mL	orange blossom water
3 cups	750 mL	all-purpose flour
½ tsp	2 mL	baking powder
½ tsp	2 mL	fine salt
¼ tsp	1 mL	ground nutmeg

DECORATION

1 lb	450 g	white rolling fondant
2 tsp	10 mL	orange blossom water
		egg white, or meringue powder with a little water, for brushing
		food colouring paste, available at cake supply stores
		icing sugar, for rolling

NOTES

◇ Orange blossom water is not as intensely fragrant as rosewater. It was my very first perfume as a child.

◇ When purchasing your essences, be sure to check that they are usable for food, and not just aromatherapy. It will state so clearly on the label.

◇ Food colouring paste holds its colour better than liquid colours, and the pastes come in an extensive selection of colour tones.

Definitely get the kids involved in this project — everyone can decorate their own springtime flowers. The subtlety of orange blossom water adds an appropriate fragrance to these flower-shaped cookies. See photo, page 32.

◇ ◇ ◇

FOR COOKIES, beat butter and sugar with electric beaters until light and fluffy, about 2 minutes. Add egg, vanilla and orange blossom water and beat well. In a separate bowl, stir flour, baking powder, salt and nutmeg. Add to butter mixture and beat on low speed just until blended. Shape dough into 2 disks, wrap and chill for at least 2 hours.

Preheat oven to 350°F (180°C) and line a baking tray with parchment paper.

On a lightly floured surface, roll out dough to ¼ inch (5 mm) and cut out flower shapes. Place cookies on baking tray, 1 inch (2.5 cm) apart and bake for 8 to 10 minutes, until just lightly browned around the edges. Allow to cool completely before icing.

FOR DECORATION, knead fondant to soften. Add orange blossom water and knead into fondant. Break fondant into pieces, keeping each wrapped at all times. Add just a touch of desired colour to a piece of fondant and knead in with your fingers, adjusting colour if necessary. Repeat with other pieces of fondant.

On a surface lightly dusted with icing sugar, roll out fondant to ⅛ inch (3 mm) thick. Using the same cookie cutter as you used for the cookies, cut out a few flower shapes. Brush a little egg white or meringue powder mixture onto the back of the fondant flower and adhere to each cookie. Cut out a small circle of fondant for centre of each flower and adhere with egg white to cookie. Let completed cookies dry for an hour, then store in an airtight container or package in cellophane bags and tie with a ribbon.

Pure and clean, white desserts have a beautiful brightness to them. Although the key ingredient in each of the desserts in this chapter may be white, sometimes the end result is a deeper, more decadent hue.

Another observation—white dessert ingredients are a lot easier to clean up than sticky caramel or melted chocolate desserts!

white

MARSHMALLOW | MERINGUE | ICING SUGAR | CRÈME FRAÎCHE
CONDENSED MILK | SOFT CHEESES

Marshmallow

Marshmallows may make us think of our childhood, and there is absolutely nothing wrong with that. As a fireside treat or when made from scratch, marshmallows are fluffy, fat-free delights for the child in each of us.

S'mores Bars

14 to 16	14 to 16	whole graham crackers
3/4 cup	175 mL	unsalted butter
2/3 cup	150 mL	light brown sugar, packed
1/2 cup	125 mL	2% milk
1/2 tsp	2 mL	vanilla extract
1 1/4 cups	300 mL	graham cracker crumbs
2 1/2 cups	625 mL	semi-sweet or milk chocolate chunks
3 cups	750 mL	mini marshmallows

S'mores may have been your campfire favourite as a child, but these bars will now be your current top pick away from the bonfire.

❖ ❖ ❖

Preheat oven to 350°F (180°C) and grease a 9-inch (2.5-L) square pan. Line the pan with parchment paper so that the paper hangs over two sides of the pan. Line bottom of pan with a single layer of whole graham crackers (about 4 ½ crackers). In a saucepan, melt butter and stir in brown sugar, milk and vanilla until dissolved. Remove from heat and stir in graham cracker crumbs (this will make a soft paste). Spread half of graham mixture over crackers in the pan. Sprinkle with a third of the chocolate chunks and half of the marshmallows. Top marshmallows with another layer of whole graham crackers and spread remaining graham mixture over top. Top with another third of chocolate chunks and remaining marshmallows. Finish with a last sprinkle of chocolate chunks and bake for 12 minutes, until marshmallows have browned. Cool completely before slicing.

S'mores Bars can be stored in an airtight container for 3 days.

NOTES

❖ These bars may sound over-the-top sweet, but surprisingly they are not. I favour using milk chocolate chunks or chips, but semi-sweet is still delicious.

❖ The vanilla graham cracker crumb mixture is what binds everything together in these layered bars; it gently softens the graham cracker layers just enough that they are easy to slice.

[Switch Up]
Warm S'mores with Ice Cream

Bring this great treat even closer to the campfire by warming them and let them ooze over a bowl of ice cream.

❖ ❖ ❖

Prepare S'mores Bars (page 23) and cut into squares.

Preheat oven to 350°F (180°C) and place squares on a parchment-lined baking sheet. Warm squares for 10 minutes, to melt chocolate chunks and soften marshmallows.

Scoop spoonfuls of checkerboard ice cream into bowls and arrange warm, gooey squares on top.

S'mores Bars

Rocky Road Truffle Cake

BROWNIE LAYER

2 1/2 ounces	75 g	bittersweet chocolate, chopped
1 1/2 cups + 1 Tbsp	375 mL + 15 mL	unsalted butter at room temperature
2/3 cup	150 mL	sugar
2	2	large eggs
1 tsp	5 mL	vanilla extract
1/2 cup	125 mL	all-purpose flour
1/4 tsp	1 mL	fine salt
1/2 cup	125 mL	walnut halves, lightly toasted, plus extra for garnish

MARSHMALLOW LAYER

		cornstarch, for dusting
1 Tbsp + 1 1/2 tsp	22 mL	gelatin powder
1/2 cup	125 mL	cold water
1 1/4 cups	300 mL	sugar
2 Tbsp	30 mL	glucose syrup or white corn syrup
2	2	large egg whites
1/2 tsp	2 mL	vanilla extract

A homemade marshmallow layer sits atop a walnut-laden brownie. Talk about decadent.

❖ ❖ ❖

FOR BROWNIE LAYER, preheat oven to 350°F (180°C). Grease an 8-inch (20-cm) square pan and line with parchment so that the paper hangs over the sides of the pan. Melt chocolate in a bowl over a pot of gently simmering water, stirring constantly. Cool chocolate to room temperature and stir in butter by hand until smooth. Stir in sugar gently and add eggs, one at a time, until blended. Stir in vanilla. Gently mix flour and salt into chocolate base and stir in walnuts. Scrape batter into prepared pan and bake for 19 to 22 minutes, until cake takes on a dull colour and feels firm when touched. Allow to cool completely.

FOR MARSHMALLOW LAYER, line an 8-inch (20-cm) square pan with parchment and dust generously with cornstarch. Sprinkle gelatin over 1/4 cup (60 mL) of the cold water, stir and set aside for 5 minutes. Melt gelatin over low heat and keep warm. Bring remaining 1/4 cup (60 mL) water, sugar and syrup to a boil over medium-high heat and cook until sugar reaches 245°F (118°C) on a candy thermometer, about 7 minutes. While sugar is cooking, whip egg whites with electric beaters or in a mixer fitted with the whisk attachment until foamy. When sugar reaches the proper temperature, pour it carefully in a stream down the side of the bowl while mixing on medium speed. Once incorporated, pour in melted gelatin and vanilla and whip mixture on high speed until thick and white, about 4 minutes. Pour marshmallow into prepared pan, sift generously with cornstarch and let set for at least 2 hours before unmoulding.

TRUFFLE GANACHE

½ cup	125 mL	whipping cream
4 ounces	120 g	bittersweet chocolate, chopped
2 Tbsp	30 mL	unsalted butter at room temperature

FOR TRUFFLE GANACHE, heat cream to just below a simmer and pour over chopped chocolate. Let sit 1 minute, then stir slowly until evenly blended. Stir in butter until melted in. Let cool for at least 30 minutes, or chill until ready to assemble.

To assemble, remove brownie from pan in 1 piece by lifting parchment overhang. Brush top of brownie with a layer of fluid ganache (if ganache sets up, just rewarm to melt). Brush excess cornstarch off marshmallow and turn over onto brownie. Peel off parchment from marshmallow carefully. Drizzle top of cake with remaining ganache and top with walnut halves. With a hot knife, cut dessert into 9 or 16 squares and arrange on a platter.

Rocky Road Truffle Cakes will keep for 1 day refrigerated or 2 days covered at room temperature.

NOTES

✧ First time making marshmallows? Generously dusting the pan and the top of the marshmallow is important for handling it after it sets. Any excess cornstarch can be brushed off before layering it on the brownie.

✧ The glucose or corn syrup is needed to keep marshmallows that nice, squishy texture. Look for glucose at a baking supply or bulk food store (but white corn syrup works just fine).

✧ For seasonal treats, I spread the marshmallow mixture into a larger pan (9-×-13-inch/3-L) and use seasonal cookie cutters to cut out shapes—ghosts for Halloween and snowflakes for Christmas.

Meringue

When I think of white desserts, meringue immediately springs to mind. Ethereal and splendid, a good meringue melts on the tip of your tongue, just teasing you to take another bite.

Raspberry Meringue Fools

SERVES 8

MERINGUE COOKIES

3 | 3	egg whites, room temperature
½ tsp | 2 mL	cream of tartar
¾ cup | 175 mL	sugar

RASPBERRY FOOL

2 cups | 500 mL	fresh raspberries
5 Tbsp | 75 mL	sugar
1½ cups | 375 mL	whipping cream
3 Tbsp | 45 mL	sour cream
1 tsp | 5 mL	finely grated orange zest
	icing sugar, for dusting

NOTES

✧ I wish I had a secret for baking meringues on a rainy or humid day, but sadly I don't. Any winter day, or a clear, dry summer day is best for a crisp meringue.

✧ Egg whites whip to fuller volume at room temperature. Warm the eggs in their shells in hot tap water before separating.

✧ Many people let their meringues dry in their gas oven overnight. Too many times I have tried this only to open the oven door to browned meringues the next morning. Now I follow the steps in this recipe so I can keep an eye on my meringues.

This is a tasty, fresh, mousse-like dessert that teases the palate with a little bit of everything scrumptious—tasty fruit, creamy whipped cream, and the crunch of meringue.

✧ ✧ ✧

FOR MERINGUE COOKIES, preheat oven to 225°F (110°C). Whip egg whites with cream of tartar until foamy. While whipping, gradually add sugar and whip on one speed lower than highest (for a tighter, more stable meringue) until whites hold a stiff peak. Whites with this much sugar will not overwhip, so give it the time it needs, about 5 minutes. Transfer meringue to a piping bag fitted with a large (#4) star tip and pipe sixteen 2-inch (5-cm) round "cookies" on a parchment-lined baking sheet. Place on centre rack of oven and bake for 1½ hours, then turn off oven and leave cookies in until dry (they should lift easily off the parchment). Let cool to room temperature.

FOR RASPBERRY FOOL, crush 1 cup (250 mL) of raspberries with 3 Tbsp (45 mL) of the sugar and set aside. Whip cream to medium peaks and whip in remaining 2 Tbsp (30 mL) sugar, sour cream and orange zest. Fold in crushed raspberries roughly (they don't have to be fully incorporated). Immediately before serving, crumble meringue cookies into raspberry fool and spoon into serving glasses.

Raspberry Meringue Sandwiches MAKES 8 SANDWICHES

These little sandwiches are great to pick up and eat with your fingers. They're a lovely addition to a shower or luncheon dessert table.

✧ ✧ ✧

Prepare Meringue Cookies and Raspberry Fool (filling) as on page 28.

TO SERVE, spoon a dollop of raspberry fool between the two meringue cookies and place on a serving plate. Assemble immediately before serving.

Lemon Meringue Pie

CRUST

1½ cups	375 mL	all-purpose flour
1 Tbsp	15 mL	sugar
½ tsp	2 mL	fine salt
⅔ cup	150 mL	unsalted butter, diced and chilled
1	1	large egg
1 Tbsp	15 mL	lemon juice

FILLING

1¼ cups	300 mL	sugar
1½ cups	375 mL	water
5 Tbsp	75 mL	cornstarch
5	5	large egg yolks
pinch	pinch	fine salt
1 Tbsp	15 mL	finely grated lemon zest
½ cup	125 mL	fresh lemon juice
2 Tbsp	30 mL	unsalted butter

Truly a classic recipe—a traditional flaky pie crust, tart lemon filling, and soft meringue peaked on top. Yum.

◇ ◇ ◇

FOR CRUST, combine flour, sugar and salt. Cut in chilled butter until mixture has a rough crumbly texture and little bits of butter are still visible. In a small bowl, whisk egg and lemon juice. Pour all at once into flour mixture and combine just until dough comes together. Shape dough into a disk and chill for at least one hour.

Preheat oven to 400°F (200°C). On a lightly floured surface, roll out dough to just less than ¼ inch (5 mm) thick. Sprinkle a 9-inch (23-cm) pie pan with flour and line with dough. Tuck in rough edges and crimp (pinch) with your fingers. Put pie shell in freezer for 10 minutes to rest and firm up. Once chilled, cover pastry with aluminum foil (allow foil to hang over crust edges to protect it) and weigh down with pie weights, dried beans or raw rice. Bake for 10 minutes, then reduce oven temperature to 375°F (190°C) and bake 15 minutes more. Remove aluminum foil and weights and bake 10 minutes more, to dry out centre of shell. Cool completely before filling.

FOR FILLING, whisk sugar, water and cornstarch in a heavy-bottomed saucepan. Whisk in egg yolks and salt and cook over low heat for 5 minutes, whisking constantly. Increase heat to medium and, still whisking, cook until filling becomes glossy and thick, about 5 more minutes. Remove from heat and strain. Stir in salt, lemon zest, lemon juice and butter until butter dissolves. Pour immediately into cooled pie shell and let cool 15 minutes. Chill completely before finishing with meringue, about 4 hours.

MERINGUE

5	5	large egg whites
½ tsp	2 mL	cream of tartar
5 Tbsp	75 mL	sugar
1 Tbsp	15 mL	cornstarch

FOR MERINGUE, preheat oven to 350°F (180°C). Whip egg whites with cream of tartar until foamy. While whipping, gradually pour in sugar and whip on one speed less than highest until whites hold a stiff peak (the meringue stands upright when whisk is lifted). Whisk in cornstarch and dollop over chilled lemon filling. Use sweeping motions with your spatula to create swirls and peaks that look so enticing once browned. Bake pie for 10 minutes, just until meringue browns lightly. Let pie cool or chill until ready to slice.

NOTES

✧ Please use real, freshly squeezed lemons for this recipe — it makes such a difference in the final result.

✧ It may seem funny to make the lemon pie filling on the stove without adding the lemon juice, but by adding the lemon juice after, you retain that fresh lemon flavour.

✧ That little measure of cornstarch in the meringue helps keep it tender and soft, and helps prevent the meringue from slipping a bit when it sits in the fridge.

✧ The other key to a meringue that does not sweat or bead on top is to be sure to avoid overwhipping the whites. One speed less than the highest gives a finer structure and you'll be less likely to overwhip.

Decorated Icing Sugar Cookies, Flower Party Cookies, Iced Gingerbread Cookies

Icing Sugar

Icing sugar is a pastry chef's saviour. It dresses up plain desserts with just a little dusting, and it can disguise rough edges or a cake that may have spent just that minute too long in the oven. It melts away to nothing when dissolved and is the base for so many delicious frostings and glazes.

Icing Sugar Cookies

MAKES ABOUT 4 DOZEN

1¼ cups	300 mL	unsalted butter at room temperature
2½ cups	625 mL	icing sugar, sifted
5	5	large egg yolks
1 tsp	5 mL	vanilla extract
½ tsp	2 mL	almond extract (optional)
3¼ cups	800 mL	pastry flour, sifted
½ tsp	2 mL	fine salt

NOTES

❖ Dusting your rolling surface with icing sugar instead of flour will allow you to get a few more "re-rolls" out of the dough—icing sugar melts into the dough, while flour, after a while, will be absorbed into the dough and toughen it up.

❖ Using egg yolks rather than whole eggs ensures a very tender dough—yolks are like butter, they add richness (fat). The whites of eggs add set and crispness (protein).

❖ The icing for these cookies is a "flood" icing. By piping an edge of icing around the outside edge of the cookie, you create a border. Inside the border you can swirl and spread the icing to your heart's content. Not happy with the result? Eat the evidence!

This cookie is a classic sablé recipe—the icing sugar gives it a tender, sandy texture that melts on your tongue.

❖ ❖ ❖

Cream butter by hand or with a mixer fitted with the paddle attachment until light and fluffy. Add icing sugar and cream until smooth. Add egg yolks slowly to butter mixture and blend until smooth. Stir in vanilla and almond extract (if using). Add pastry flour and salt and combine until dough comes together. Shape into a disk, wrap and chill for at least 2 hours before rolling.

Preheat oven to 325°F (160°C). On a surface lightly dusted with icing sugar, knead dough slightly to soften (this will prevent cracking as it is rolled. Roll out dough to ¼ inch (5 mm) thick and cut out desired shapes. Unused dough can be re-rolled and cut again (just chill for a few minutes if it becomes too soft). Place cutouts an inch (2.5 cm) apart on a greased or parchment-lined baking sheet and bake on the centre rack of the oven for 10 to 12 minutes, until bottom of cookies turn a light golden brown. Remove cookies from pan to a cooling rack and cool completely.

[Switch Up]
Decorated Icing Sugar Cookies

ROYAL ICING

MAKES 1½ CUPS (375 ML)

3 Tbsp | 45 mL	meringue powder (available at cake stores and bulk stores)
½ cup | 125 mL	warm water
4½ cups | 1125 mL	icing sugar, sifted
1 tsp | 5 mL	vanilla extract
½ tsp | 2 mL	cream of tartar
	food colouring, as needed

Prepare and cool Icing Sugar Cookies (page 33).

FOR ICING, stir all ingredients to blend, then beat with electric mixer on high speed until mixture is stiff, about 7 minutes. Tint portions of icing as desired. To store, keep icing tightly covered, with plastic wrap resting directly on surface of icing.

To create a satiny-finished cookie, thin the icing a little by adding water, a few drops at a time, until desired consistency is achieved. First pipe an outline of icing around edge of cookie with ⅛-inch (3-mm) plain tip. Using a brush, fill in cookie with icing (it's just like colouring inside the lines). For a colourful swirl effect, add drops of a contrasting colour on the cookie and swirl in with a toothpick. For a textured contrast, let royal icing dry completely, then pipe on top.

White Chocolate Cloud Cake

CAKE

9 ounces	270 g	white chocolate, chopped
1/2 cup	125 mL	unsalted butter
2	2	whole large eggs
4	4	large eggs, separated
1/2 cup	125 mL	icing sugar, sifted
2 tsp	10 mL	finely grated lemon zest

TOPPING

1 1/2 cups	375 mL	whipping cream
1/4 cup	60 mL	icing sugar
1 Tbsp	15 mL	skim milk powder
1 tsp	5 mL	vanilla extract
2 cups	500 mL	fresh strawberries, hulled and halved or quartered
		icing sugar and white chocolate shavings, for garnish

NOTES

✧ You'll admire as the cake comes out of the oven how beautifully it has souffléd. Soon after it will begin to fall, but don't be distraught—it's supposed to. This leaves more room for cream and berries after it's cooled.

✧ White chocolate is ideal for making chocolate shavings. It's much softer than dark chocolate, and a few strokes with a vegetable peeler over the chocolate and you'll feel like a pro.

Wow—a flourless white chocolate cake! Icing sugar's fine texture really works to make this rich cake seem tender and light.

✧ ✧ ✧

FOR CAKE, preheat oven to 350°F (180°C) and line the bottom of an ungreased 9-inch (23-cm) springform pan with parchment paper.

Melt chopped white chocolate in a microwave on medium heat, stirring every 10 seconds until melted. Cut butter into pieces and set on top. Cover dish and allow to melt in while preparing eggs. Whip whole eggs, egg yolks and 1/4 cup (60 mL) of icing sugar with electric beaters until pale and fluffy. Stir chocolate mixture to incorporate butter and fold into egg mixture. Stir in lemon zest. In a separate bowl, whip whites with remaining icing sugar until they hold a medium peak (bend slightly when beaters are lifted). Fold a third of whites into chocolate mixture and then fold in remaining two-thirds. Spread into prepared pan and bake for 35 to 45 minutes, until top of cake is an even golden brown colour. Let cake cool completely. Don't worry if it falls in the centre—it's supposed to. To remove, gently run a knife around the outside edge of the cake and remove springform ring. Peel off parchment and gently place on a platter.

FOR TOPPING, whip cream with icing sugar until it holds a medium peak. Fold in skim milk powder and vanilla. Spoon over cake. Arrange strawberries on top and dust generously with icing sugar before serving. To create white chocolate shavings, use a vegetable peeler to scrape curls or shavings of white chocolate from a large piece (the softer the chocolate, the bigger the shavings).

Cake can be made a day in advance and can be assembled up to 6 hours ahead of serving.

Crème Fraîche

The English translation of crème fraîche is "fresh cream," but actually it is very rich soured cream. For the recipes in this section, I provide instructions for making your own crème fraîche at home, if it's not available in your local grocery (or check out a cheese shop). If neither of these options is available to you, please feel confident that using full-fat sour cream will give you perfect results.

Crème Fraîche

2 Tbsp | 30 mL   buttermilk
2 cups | 500 mL   whipping cream

Stir buttermilk into whipping cream and pour into a plastic or glass container such as a juice pitcher and cover with plastic wrap. Place pitcher in a larger container, and pour hot tap water around the pitcher, filling up to the height of the cream. Place container in a warm, draft-free spot (I find on top of the fridge is best) and let sit for 24 to 48 hours (it ripens faster in summer than winter).

To determine if set, jiggle the container slightly—the cream should not shift and should have a sweet, lemony smell. Chill completely. Spoon crème fraîche off the top, being careful not to stir in the liquid whey, which will settle at the bottom of the container. Crème fraîche will keep as long as the expiry date on the cream used to make it.

Lemon Cake Cookies

COOKIES

½ cup + 1 Tbsp	140 mL	unsalted butter at room temperature
1 cup + 2 Tbsp	280 mL	sugar
1 Tbsp	15 mL	finely grated lemon zest
2	2	large egg yolks
1	1	whole large egg
1¼ cups	300 mL	crème fraîche (page 36) or sour cream
2½ cups	625 mL	pastry flour
¾ tsp	4 mL	baking powder
¾ tsp	4 mL	baking soda
½ tsp	2 mL	fine salt

ICING

1½ cups	375 mL	icing sugar, sifted
2 Tbsp	30 mL	fresh lemon juice
3 Tbsp	45 mL	unsalted butter, melted

These cookies are tender and light, and sort of like a cupcake without the paper cup. They are a real weakness for me—I can hardly eat just one.

✧ ✧ ✧

FOR COOKIES, beat butter and sugar together until light and fluffy and stir in lemon zest. Beat in egg yolks and whole egg until fully incorporated. Stir in crème fraîche or sour cream until smooth. In a separate bowl, sift flour, baking powder, baking soda and salt. Add to wet ingredients and stir just until blended. Chill batter for 30 minutes, to set butter a little.

Preheat oven to 325°F (160°C). Spoon tablespoons of batter (an ice cream scoop works great) onto a parchment-lined cookie sheet, leaving 2 inches (5 cm) between cookies. Bake for 15 to 18 minutes, just until the bottoms of the cookies turn golden brown. Remove to a cooling rack and cool before icing.

FOR ICING, stir sifted icing sugar into lemon juice until smooth. Stir in melted butter (this will thicken the icing a bit). Dip the tops of the cookies into icing, and place on a cooling rack, so excess icing can drip off. Let cookies set 1 hour before storing in an airtight container, with layers of parchment between the cookies to prevent sticking.

NOTES

✧ The difference between sour cream and crème fraîche? About 21% milk fat. Regular sour cream is 14% m.f., while crème fraîche is made from whipping cream at 35% m.f. or sometimes even higher.

✧ I make an autumn version of this cookie using browned butter and country spices (cinnamon, nutmeg, etc.) I can't decide which is my favourite.

[Switch Up]

Lemon Cake Cookie Sandwiches

LEMON CURD

MAKES 1 CUP (250 ML)

1/3 cup	75 mL	fresh lemon juice
3	3	large eggs
1	1	large egg yolk
1/2 cup	125 mL	sugar
1/2 cup	125 mL	unsalted butter, cut into pieces
1 tsp	5 mL	lemon zest

These cookies make for great ice cream sandwiches, too, filled with lemon ice or Lemon Ice Cream (page 178).

❖ ❖ ❖

Prepare and cool Lemon Cake Cookies (page 37).

FOR LEMON CURD, whisk together lemon juice, eggs and yolk, and sugar. Whisk in butter and add lemon zest. Place bowl over a pot of simmering water and whisk steadily but gently, until curd becomes thick and pale and creamy, about 10 to 15 minutes. Remove from heat and chill before using. Lemon curd will keep for 5 days in an airtight container.

To assemble, spread a little lemon curd on base of one cookie and sandwich with a second. Chill until ready to serve.

New York Style Cheesecake

CRUST

1/2 cup	125 mL	unsalted butter, room temperature
1/4 cup	60 mL	light brown sugar, packed
1	1	large egg
1 1/4 cups	300 mL	all-purpose flour

FILLING

2 lb (4 pkg)	1 kg	cream cheese, room temperature
1 1/4 cups	300 mL	sugar
1/4 cup	60 mL	all-purpose flour
3	3	large eggs
1 Tbsp	15 mL	vanilla extract
1/2 cup	125 mL	crème fraîche (page 36) or sour cream

TOPPING

1 1/2 cups	375 mL	crème fraîche or sour cream
1/4 cup	60 mL	sugar
1 tsp	5 mL	vanilla extract

NOTES

❖ If you are looking for crème fraîche in the dairy section of the grocery, look not just where the sour cream is located, but near the cream cheese or high-end yogurts. That's where I seem to find it.

❖ The crust for this cheesecake is interesting—not your typical graham crust. I find the two-step method of first baking half the pie-dough-style crust then pressing the remaining raw dough over it, creates a sublime, almost crustless cheesecake.

❖ Gradual cooling is key to a cheesecake that does not crack. Don't rush to put it in the fridge—make sure it cools completely to room temperature before chilling it.

❖ Running a knife around the outside of the cheesecake before it cools completely will also help prevent cracking.

Like the Lemon Meringue Pie (page 30), this is another of the "great" recipes, a must-have for your dessert collection. Simplicity is key here—you don't want to mask the fine taste and texture of this cheesecake under an oozing of caramel sauce or another fancy concoction. Just a few select berries will accent this dessert perfectly.

❖ ❖ ❖

FOR CRUST, preheat oven to 350°F (180°C). Beat butter and brown sugar until light and fluffy. Beat in egg until smooth. Stir in flour and mix until dough comes together. Divide dough in half; wrap one half and chill, then spread the other half of the dough onto the bottom of an ungreased 10-inch (25-cm) springform pan (it will cover the bottom of the pan very thinly). Bake for 10 minutes and allow to cool. Once cooled, press the other half of the dough onto the first layer. Don't worry if dough seems uneven—it will all even out in the end. Do not bake second layer.

FOR FILLING, increase oven temperature to 450°F (230°C). Beat cream cheese until very fluffy and smooth, scraping down the sides of the bowl often. Gradually add sugar while beating, continuing to scrape down the sides of the bowl often. Beat in flour. Add eggs one at a time, waiting until egg is fully incorporated before adding next. Beat in vanilla and 1/2 cup (125 mL) crème fraîche or sour cream. Scrape batter onto crust base and bake for 10 minutes. Reduce oven temperature to 300°F (150°C) and bake for 30 minutes.

While cheesecake is baking, prepare topping, Stir crème fraîche or sour cream, sugar and vanilla together until sugar dissolves. Remove cheesecake from oven carefully and gently spread crème fraîche topping over cheesecake, taking care not to tear the surface of the cheesecake. Return to oven and bake 15 minutes. Cool cheesecake for 30 minutes, then run a spatula or knife gently around the edge of cheesecake to loosen (this will prevent any cracking). Cool cheesecake to room temperature and chill overnight.

To serve, remove springform pan ring and slice with a hot, dry knife. Serve with fresh berries.

Condensed Milk

Ooey, gooey goodness—condensed milk is the secret behind so many decadent bars, squares and candies. My mom never baked with condensed milk, so it is a relatively new ingredient for me to play with, and I'm hooked.

Gooey Southern Squares

MAKES ONE 9-INCH (2.5-L) SQUARE PAN
18 TO 36 SQUARES

2 cups | 500 mL	digestive cookie crumbs (about 20)
1 cup | 250 mL	unsalted butter, melted
1 cup | 250 mL	salted roasted peanuts
1½ cups | 375 mL	white chocolate chips
1 cup | 250 mL	unsweetened flaked coconut, lightly toasted
2 | 2	14-ounce (398-mL) tins condensed milk

NOTES

✧ For the best-tasting squares, be sure to use salted roasted peanuts. That combination of sweet and salt is just too delectable.

✧ The digestive cookies make a tasty base for these squares, and very tender, too. Try using a different cookie, like oatmeal or gingersnap, for your own twist.

✧ To get every bit of goodness from your can of condensed milk, immerse it in hot water for a few minutes before opening.

✧ Replacing the peanuts with macadamia nuts in the Switch-Up is a great idea. Try almonds or hazelnuts, too. I've tried and love them all.

You may recognize these squares as a version of Hello Dollies. They're so easy to assemble, and so difficult to resist.

✧ ✧ ✧

Preheat oven to 325°F (160°C) and grease a 9-inch (2.5-L) square pan. Line pan with parchment so paper overhangs on two sides (this allows you to pull out squares easily for slicing).

For base, pulse digestive cookies to a fine crumb in a food processor. Toss with melted butter to combine and press into prepared pan. Sprinkle peanuts over base. Sprinkle chocolate chips over peanuts, then top with toasted coconut. Pour condensed milk over coconut and spread gently. Bake for 55 to 65 minutes, until condensed milk is bubbling and a golden brown. Allow to cool completely (about 3 hours) before slicing.

Store Gooey Southern Squares in an airtight container for up to a week.

Switch Up
Gooey Down Under Slices

I take this square even deeper south to Australia. Serve a wedge of this with a scoop of coconut ice cream, and you've found heaven.

✧ ✧ ✧

Prepare Gooey Southern Squares (page 40), except make them in a 9-inch (23-cm) round springform pan and replace peanuts with macadamia nuts. After cooled, drizzle melted dark chocolate over tart and cut into wedges to serve.

Dulce de Leche Mini Tortes

FILLING

2	2	14-ounce (398-mL) tins condensed milk
1 Tbsp	15 mL	vanilla extract

LAYERS

2 cups	500 mL	all-purpose flour
3 Tbsp	45 mL	sugar
1 tsp	5 mL	baking powder
1/4 tsp	1 mL	fine salt
3/4 cup	175 mL	vegetable shortening
1/4 cup	60 mL	2% milk
		icing sugar, for dusting

NOTES

◇ These mini tortes are based on Alfajores, a traditional South American sandwich cookie filled with dulce de leche. I adopted this particular recipe from my friend Pierro, a talented young chef whose roots are Peruvian.

◇ While I normally don't bake with shortening, this recipe does work best using it, both for the light colour and the tender texture. With all that caramel filling, it certainly does melt in your mouth.

◇ It's best to make your dulce de leche filling a day ahead—it takes a long time to cool to spreadable consistency. Chilled, this gooey caramel keeps for weeks.

Dulce de Leche is a South American decadence. Traditionally, milk and sugar are slowly simmered until reduced to a rich caramel spread, but making it from condensed milk gives us a shortcut.

◇ ◇ ◇

FOR FILLING, scrape condensed milk into a heavy-bottomed saucepan. Bring to a simmer over medium heat, stirring constantly. Continue to cook until milk thickens and becomes a rich caramel colour, stirring constantly (I switch between a whisk and heatproof spatula). This takes about 20 minutes. Remove from heat and scrape into a heatproof bowl. Stir in vanilla and allow to cool to room temperature.

FOR LAYERS, preheat oven to 350°F (180°C). Combine flour, sugar, baking powder and salt. Cut in shortening until dough is an even crumbly texture. Add milk and combine until dough comes together. Shape dough into a disk, wrap and set aside to rest for 20 minutes.

On a lightly floured surface, roll out pastry to 1/4 inch (5 mm) thick and cut out 24 disks 1 1/2 inches (3.5 cm) across. Place disks on a parchment-lined baking sheet and prick with a fork. Bake for about 6 minutes, until they brown just slightly on the bottom, but have no colour on top. Allow to cool.

To assemble, spread a generous spoonful of dulce de leche filling on a cookie and top with another, pressing gently. Repeat layers, so that each torte has four cookies and three layers of filling. Top with a generous dusting of icing sugar and chill until ready to serve.

These tortes are great made at least a day ahead and refrigerated, to soften. They can also be frozen.

Soft Cheeses

Fresh cheese in desserts certainly extends beyond cream cheese. Anything dairy seems to make for a perfect ending to a meal. I even love just a piece of brie with some fruit to finish my glass of wine. But here, baked into desserts, fresh cheese takes on a different personality.

Ricotta Custards

SERVES 4

1 1/2 cups	375 mL	fresh ricotta cheese (regular, not low-fat)
1/4 cup	60 mL	sugar
2	2	large eggs
1	1	vanilla bean
pinch	pinch	ground cinnamon

Simple and sweet, served warm from the oven or chilled, these custards hit the spot.

❖ ❖ ❖

Preheat oven to 350°F (180°C). Beat ricotta with sugar until smooth. Whisk eggs separately to combine and then whisk into ricotta. Scrape seeds from vanilla bean into cheese mixture and whisk in with cinnamon. Spoon ricotta into four 5-ounce (165-mL) ramekins and place on a baking sheet. Bake for 30 to 40 minutes, until tops are a deep golden brown.

NOTES

❖ Any cheese not aged is considered a soft or fresh cheese. This includes cream cheese, mascarpone, ricotta, chèvre frais, quark and even yogurt.

❖ This is one of a very few custard recipes that can be baked without a water bath and that makes this an even simpler recipe.

❖ Spark up this custard with a little lemon or lime zest — or how about a little jam spooned into the bottom?

[Switch Up]
Ricotta Custards with Cherry Compote

CHERRY COMPOTE

MAKES 2 CUPS (500 ML)

2 cups	500 mL	red wine
3	3	black peppercorns
1/2 cup	125 mL	sugar
1/4 cup	60 mL	white corn syrup
		lemon juice (optional)
2 cups	500 mL	pitted tart cherries

A quick dress-up of wine-poached cherries makes these custards perfect for entertaining. If cherries aren't in season, use plums, peaches or even sliced pears.

✧ ✧ ✧

Prepare Ricotta Custards (page 43).

For compote, simmer all ingredients in a saucepan over medium-low heat until sauce reduces by about half and doesn't run when dripped onto a plate, about 10 minutes. Allow to cool to room temperature. Spoon over ricotta custards and serve.

Goat Cheese Pineapple Tart

CRUST

6 ounces	180 g	fresh goat cheese
1/3 cup	75 mL	unsalted butter, room temperature
1 1/2 cups	375 mL	all-purpose flour
pinch	pinch	fine salt

FILLING

2 tsp	10 mL	cornstarch
1/2 cup	125 mL	whipping cream
1 Tbsp	15 mL	golden corn syrup
1/4 cup	60 mL	sugar
1/4 cup	60 mL	dark brown sugar, packed
3	3	large egg yolks
2 Tbsp	30 mL	unsalted butter
1 tsp	5 mL	vanilla extract
pinch	pinch	fine salt
3/4 cup	175 mL	unsweetened coconut

TOPPING

2 cups	500 mL	golden pineapple, sliced
1/4 cup	60 mL	dark brown sugar, packed
4 ounces	120 g	fresh goat cheese
1 tsp	5 mL	crushed pink peppercorns (optional)

This is a beautiful-looking tart with such an element of surprise — between the fresh goat cheese, the sweet pineapple and the crushed pink peppercorns, you'll really impress your guests with this one. Try it after a late summer barbecue.

✧ ✧ ✧

FOR CRUST, beat goat cheese and butter until smooth. Add flour and salt and blend just until dough comes together. Shape into a disk, wrap and chill for 2 hours before rolling.

On a lightly floured surface, roll out pastry to 1/4 inch (5 mm) thickness. Line a 9-inch (23-cm) removable-bottom tart pan with pastry and chill for 15 minutes.

Preheat oven to 350°F (180°C). Line pastry shell with foil and weight with pie weights, dried beans or raw rice. Bake for 20 minutes, then remove weights and foil and bake another 10 minutes, until lightly browned. Allow to cool.

FOR FILLING, whisk cornstarch and whipping cream in a saucepan to combine. Whisk in corn syrup, both sugars and egg yolks. Cook mixture over medium heat, stirring constantly, until it thickens and becomes glossy. Remove from heat and stir in butter, vanilla and salt. Stir in coconut and chill for an hour before spreading into cooled crust.

FOR TOPPING, preheat oven to broil. Place pineapple on baking sheet and sprinkle with brown sugar. Broil 2 minutes, until sugar melts. Arrange warm pineapple over chilled filling. Crumble goat cheese over top, sprinkle with crushed pink peppercorns and serve.

NOTES

✧ The tang of goat cheese really lends itself well to this tart, both in the crust and sprinkled on top.

✧ The filling between the two goat cheese layers is sweet and gooey, kind of like a butter tart. It's a perfect foil for the slices of fresh pineapple.

✧ Pink peppercorns are from a different family and are milder than traditional black peppercorns, and complement the other flavours going on in this tart, sort of the way fresh ginger adds spice and lightens up other desserts.

Vibrant and vivacious, yellow is the light as it brightens into full morning. Yellow is when I am up early, starting a day of baking while I sip my coffee. Yellow can be mild and pale (though never bland), but it can also be lush and intense.

Yellow desserts are as enticing as the start of a new day.

yellow

APPLESAUCE | CLASSIC APPLE | CORNMEAL | BUTTER
CITRUS ZEST | TART LEMON

Applesauce

Wholesome and fresh-tasting, applesauce should not be relegated to a plate of pork chops or a lunch cup. The moisture it lends to baked goods keeps them fresh for days, and it can even allow you to reduce sugar or fat in some recipes.

Applesauce Coffee Cake

MAKES ONE 9-×5-INCH (2-L) LOAF PAN

This is a classic coffee cake—and the applesauce brings a subtle fruit taste, and a nice, easy-slicing texture.

✧ ✧ ✧

Preheat oven to 350°F (180°C) and grease and flour a 9- × 5-inch (2-L) loaf pan.

FOR LOAF, whisk vegetable oil, both sugars, whole egg, egg yolk and vanilla until smooth. Stir in applesauce. In a separate bowl, sift flour, baking powder, baking soda, nutmeg and ginger; stir gently into applesauce mixture.

FOR STREUSEL, combine sugar, flour and cinnamon. Stir in melted butter and walnut pieces, and toss to coat.

Spoon half the applesauce batter into prepared loaf pan and sprinkle with half the streusel. Top with remaining batter and sprinkle remaining streusel to finish. Bake for 40 to 50 minutes, until a tester inserted in the centre of the cake comes out clean. Cool loaf for 20 minutes, before turning out on a rack to cool completely.

LOAF

½ cup	125 mL	vegetable oil
½ cup	125 mL	sugar
⅓ cup	75 mL	light brown sugar, packed
1	1	large egg
1	1	large egg yolk
2 tsp	10 mL	vanilla extract
1 cup	250 mL	unsweetened applesauce
1⅔ cups	400 mL	pastry flour
1 tsp	5 mL	baking powder
¾ tsp	4 mL	baking soda
½ tsp	2 mL	ground nutmeg
½ tsp	2 mL	ground ginger

STREUSEL

½ cup	125 mL	light brown sugar, packed
2 Tbsp	30 mL	all-purpose flour
2 tsp	10 mL	ground cinnamon
2 Tbsp	30 mL	unsalted butter, melted
1 cup	250 mL	walnut pieces, lightly toasted

NOTES

✧ This is a perfect recipe for a novice baker, and great for kids to practise their measuring and mixing. There is very little technique here—just go to town!

✧ Do use unsweetened applesauce in these recipes for optimal results.

✧ This coffee cake is comfort food for your house—the cinnamon and applesauce fills the house with autumn fragrance.

Jumbo Applesauce Muffins

MAKES 6 JUMBO MUFFINS

Turn a break-time coffee cake into a breakfast treat by baking them into muffins. This recipe also freezes very well if you're trying to stock up.

❖ ❖ ❖

Prepare the Applesauce Coffee Cake as on page 49, except use 6 greased jumbo muffin tins instead of loaf pan, and bake for 30 to 40 minutes. Let muffins cool for 20 minutes before turning out.

Chocolate Applesauce Cake

Chocolate Applesauce Cakes

APPLESAUCE

2 cups	500 mL	peeled and diced apple, preferably Granny Smith
3 Tbsp	45 mL	sugar
1½ tsp	7 mL	unsalted butter
1 inch	2.5 cm	fresh ginger, peeled and sliced

CAKES

½ cup	125 mL	unsalted butter at room temperature
½ cup	125 mL	vegetable oil
1¾ cups	425 mL	sugar
2	2	large eggs
1 tsp	5 mL	vanilla extract
2¼ cups	310 mL	all-purpose flour
½ cup	125 mL	Dutch process cocoa powder
1 tsp	5 mL	baking soda
1 tsp	5 mL	fine salt
½ tsp	2 mL	ground cinnamon
1⅓ cups	325 mL	applesauce (as prepared above)
½ cup	125 mL	buttermilk
8 ounces	240 g	bittersweet chocolate chunks

GLAZE

¾ cup	175 mL	whipping cream
6 ounces	175 g	bittersweet chocolate, chopped
¼ cup	60 mL	unsalted butter, room temperature
		hazelnuts, toasted and peeled, for garnish

This is a fabulous, moist, rich chocolate cake recipe. Who knew applesauce could be so good?

◇ ◇ ◇

FOR APPLESAUCE, simmer diced apple, sugar, butter and ginger uncovered until tender, about 20 minutes. Remove and discard ginger. Purée sauce and chill.

FOR CAKES, preheat oven to 325°F (160°C). Grease and sugar six 1 ½ -cup (375-mL) brioche tins or 12 large muffin cups. Beat butter, oil and sugar with electric beaters until smooth. Add eggs one at a time, mixing well after each addition. Beat in vanilla. In a separate bowl, sift flour, cocoa, baking soda, salt and cinnamon. Whisk buttermilk and applesauce together. Add flour mixture to butter mixture, alternating with applesauce and mixing well after each addition. Stir in chocolate chunks. Spoon batter into prepared tins and bake for 18 to 20 minutes, until cakes spring back when pressed. Allow cakes to cool in the pan for 15 minutes, then turn out onto a rack to cool completely.

FOR GLAZE, heat cream to just below a simmer and pour over chopped chocolate. Let sit for one minute, then stir to smooth out. Stir in butter to melt in and thicken glaze. Pour over top of cakes and let drip deliciously down the sides. Top each cake with 3 hazelnuts.

Serve cakes at room temperature and store in an airtight container.

NOTES

◇ I do recommend making the applesauce from scratch for this recipe. The taste is remarkable (even on its own), and it really takes no time at all. If you'd like to use storebought, be sure to use the unsweetened.

◇ Don't want to use applesauce? The same measure of finely grated zucchini is also delicious.

◇ Granny Smith apples seems to work best for the applesauce, both in taste and colour.

◇ Greasing and sugaring the pans ensures the cakes slip out easily once they've started cooling, but the sugar also creates a pretty and tasty crust just around the edges, so that even a dusting of icing sugar would finish the cakes off nicely.

Classic Apple

I can never seem to make enough apple desserts. Here in Canada our other fruit seasons are so brief, we have to get creative with what I would call our national fruit. Here are a few staples you would expect—fabulous just about any time of year.

Apple Crumble

TOPPING

1 cup + 2 Tbsp	280 mL	unsalted butter, room temperature
¼ cup	60 mL	light brown sugar, packed
2 Tbsp	30 mL	sugar
1	1	large egg
1 tsp	5 mL	vanilla extract
1¾ cups	425 mL	all-purpose flour
¼ tsp	1 mL	fine salt
¼ tsp	1 mL	baking powder
¼ tsp	1 mL	ground nutmeg

FRUIT

10 cups	2.5 L	diced apple such as Granny Smith, Spy or Mutsu
2 Tbsp	30 mL	lemon, juiced
⅓ cup	75 mL	sugar
1 tsp	5 mL	ground cinnamon
		light brown or demerara sugar, for sprinkling

If you've made crumble even just a few times, you know you can do this with your eyes closed. Choose a pretty dish to bake it in, to dress it up.

❖ ❖ ❖

FOR TOPPING, preheat oven to 375°F (190°C). Beat butter and both sugars until light and fluffy. Beat in egg and vanilla. In a separate bowl, stir flour, salt, baking powder and nutmeg to combine. Add to butter mixture and combine just until blended. Shape into a disk, wrap and chill while preparing fruit.

FOR FRUIT, toss diced apple with lemon juice in a 10-cup (2.5-L) baking dish, then stir in sugar and cinnamon. Bake fruit for 30 minutes, then remove from oven. Grate crumble topping over apples using a cheese grater. Sprinkle crumble with brown or demerara sugar and return to oven. Bake for 30 minutes, until crumble is a rich golden brown and juices are bubbling. Serve warm with ice cream!

NOTES

❖ This is a cottage dessert for me. Our cottage kitchen is small and simple, but with some basic pantry ingredients and a trip to the farmers' market, I can throw together a tasty dessert and let it bake while I take that quiet, early autumn stroll down the beach.

❖ Using a box grater to "crumble" the topping onto the apples is simple, and looks really nice. This topping bakes up like a cookie dough—a nice complement to the apples.

❖ Pre-bake the fruit to make sure it gets nice and soft, and so it's not too wet under the crumble topping. Of course, any of your favourite fruit combinations would work here, with apples as the base—apple/cranberry, apple/rhubarb, apple/raspberry, apple/raisin.

Apple Crumble Parfait

APPLE BRANDY CUSTARD

MAKES ABOUT 1 CUP (250 ML)

1 cup	250 mL	half-and-half cream
3 Tbsp	45 mL	sugar
3	3	large egg yolks
1 tsp	5 mL	vanilla extract
1 Tbsp	15 mL	Calvados
1 cup	250 mL	whipping cream, whipped to soft peaks, lightly sweetened

Layering cooled apple crumble in a parfait glass with a custard sauce creates an autumn trifle of sorts. You can also just serve the crumble with the custard sauce drizzled on top.

❖ ❖ ❖

Prepare Apple Crumble (page 53).

FOR APPLE BRANDY CUSTARD, bring cream to just below a simmer over moderate heat. In a bowl, whisk sugar and egg yolks. Slowly pour hot cream over sugar mixture, whisking constantly. Return mixture to low heat and stir with a wooden spoon until sauce coats the spoon, about 4 minutes. Strain and stir in Calvados or other brandy. Chill completely before serving.

In small spoonfuls, layer apple crumble, custard and whipped cream in parfait glasses.

Caramel Apple Galette

CRUST

3 Tbsp	45 mL	2% milk at room temperature
1¼ tsp	6 mL	instant dry active yeast
3 Tbsp	45 mL	sugar
1¾ cups	435 mL	all-purpose flour
¾ tsp	4 mL	fine salt
2	2	large eggs
1	1	large egg yolk
½ cup	125 mL	unsalted butter, room temperature
1	1	egg mixed with 2 Tbsp (30 mL) water for egg wash

FRUIT

5	5	large Granny Smith apples, peeled and sliced
1 Tbsp	15 mL	lemon juice
¼ cup	60 mL	unsalted butter
¼ cup	60 mL	sugar
2 Tbsp	30 mL	brandy
½ tsp	2 mL	ground cinnamon

A galette is typically a rustic, free-form tart filled with a mountain of seasonal fruit. The crust of this particular galette is made with a tender, buttery brioche dough, making this quite an elegant dessert.

❖ ❖ ❖

FOR CRUST, stir together milk, yeast and sugar. In a large mixing bowl, combine flour and salt. Pour in milk mixture and add eggs and egg yolk. With electric mixer fitted with the dough attachments or in a stand-up mixer fitted with a dough hook, mix on low speed until blended. Add butter in pieces to dough and beat for 3 minutes until it's an even, silky consistency. Place dough in a large bowl, cover with plastic wrap and chill overnight.

FOR FRUIT, toss apple slices in lemon juice. Heat butter and sugar over high heat in a sauté pan until bubbling. Add apples and sauté until nicely browned, about 10 minutes. Stir in brandy and cinnamon.

Preheat oven to 350°F (180°C). Place ring of 10-inch (25-cm) springform pan on baking sheet lined with parchment.

On a lightly floured surface, roll dough into a 14-inch (35-cm) circle and place in springform ring. The extra will overlap 2 inches (5 cm) on the ring. Spoon in apples and fold edge back over filling. Brush dough with egg wash. Bake for 25 minutes, until edges of tart are richly browned. Let cool for an hour before unmoulding and slicing.

NOTES

❖ If you've never made bread before, brioche is that place to start. It is a very forgiving dough, and not at all temperamental — it can even be mixed in a bowl by hand. You do need to let it sit overnight in the fridge, though, so that it can be handled easily when rolling.

❖ This is a perfect brunch tart — serve it at the beginning as a breakfast tart, or let it be your dessert.

❖ For a richer dessert, serve this galette with the Apple Brandy Custard (page 54).

Cornmeal

You may have noticed that I love cornmeal—I'll sneak a little bit into a pie crust for colour and texture, into a coffee cake for tenderness, and into biscotti for contrast. It must be my Southern roots showing.

Cornmeal Muffins

MUFFINS

1¹/₃ cups	325 mL	buttermilk
¹/₃ cup	75 mL	vegetable oil
2	2	large eggs
3 Tbsp	45 mL	sugar
1 Tbsp	15 mL	fresh lime juice
1 cup	250 mL	cornmeal
1 cup	250 mL	all-purpose flour
2 tsp	10 mL	finely grated lime zest
1 tsp	5 mL	baking soda
1 tsp	5 mL	fine salt

GLAZE

1¹/₂ cups	375 mL	icing sugar, sifted
2 Tbsp	30 mL	fresh lime juice
¹/₂ tsp	2 mL	finely grated lime zest

If you can, please enjoy these fresh out of the oven, absolutely slathered with warm butter and maybe a little jam.

✧ ✧ ✧

FOR MUFFINS, preheat oven to 375°F (190°C) and grease a muffin tin. Whisk buttermilk, oil, eggs, sugar and lime juice to combine. In a separate bowl, stir together cornmeal, flour, lime zest, baking soda and salt. Add to buttermilk mixture and whisk until smooth (batter will be very fluid). Pour or spoon batter into greased muffin cups, filling ¾ full. Bake for 15 to 18 minutes, until tops are lightly golden brown and muffin springs back when touched.

FOR GLAZE, whisk icing sugar, lime juice and zest until smooth. Brush or drizzle over muffins.

Cornmeal muffins are best served warm, but these keep well for a day in an airtight container, or can be frozen and reheated.

NOTES

✧ Yum, yum, yum…these truly are my favourite muffins. They're not terribly sweet, so I dress them up for dinner by omitting the glaze and stirring in diced pepper, onion, cooked bacon and/or ¹/₃ cup (75 mL) grated cheddar cheese.

✧ If you don't have buttermilk kicking around, use ²/₃ cup (150 mL) 2% milk and ²/₃ cup (150 mL) plain yogurt.

✧ I also bake this recipe as a cornbread, in a seasoned 8-inch (20-cm) skillet. You can even bake it on the barbecue, with the lid down on medium heat for about 20 minutes. Perfect with ribs.

Blueberry Cornmeal Loaves with Orange Butter   MAKES 8 MINI LOAVES

ORANGE BUTTER

MAKES ½ CUP (125 mL)

½ cup	125 mL	unsalted butter at room temperature
1 Tbsp	15 mL	honey
2 tsp	10 mL	finely grated orange zest

I love making flavoured butters — it's an easy way to dress up simple breakfast baked goods.

◇ ◇ ◇

FOR ORANGE BUTTER, beat soft butter with honey and orange zest. Chill until ready to serve.

Prepare Cornmeal Muffins recipe (page 56), except stir in 1 cup (250 mL) fresh blueberries. Divide between 8 greased mini loaf pans and bake for 17 to 20 minutes, until top springs back when touched. Serve warm with Orange Butter.

Lemon Cornmeal Waffles with Strawberry Rhubarb Syrup

Lemon Cornmeal Waffles with Strawberry Rhubarb Syrup

MAKES 12 WAFFLES
SERVES 6

STRAWBERRY RHUBARB SYRUP

2 cups	500 mL	diced fresh or frozen rhubarb
2 cups	500 mL	quartered fresh strawberries
1 cup	250 mL	sugar
1/2 cup	125 mL	white corn syrup
1 cup	250 mL	water
1	1	vanilla bean

WAFFLES

1 1/4 cups	300 mL	all-purpose flour
1/2 cup	125 mL	cornmeal
2 Tbsp	30 mL	sugar
1 Tbsp	15 mL	baking powder
2 tsp	10 mL	lemon zest
1/2 tsp	2 mL	fine salt
1 1/4 cups	300 mL	buttermilk
1/2 cup	125 mL	vegetable oil
2	2	large eggs, separated

GARNISH

1 cup	250 mL	whipping cream
2 Tbsp	30 mL	sugar
1 cup	250 mL	quartered fresh strawberries
		icing sugar, for dusting

Another great idea for a brunch dessert. Instead of starting your brunch with waffles, finish it with waffles.

✧ ✧ ✧

FOR STRAWBERRY RHUBARB SYRUP, bring diced rhubarb, 1 cup (250 mL) of the strawberries, sugar, corn syrup, water and seeds scraped from vanilla bean to a simmer. Gently simmer for 10 minutes until rhubarb is tender and colour is extracted. Remove from heat and strain. Stir in remaining quartered strawberries while warm and let cool.

FOR WAFFLES, stir flour, cornmeal, sugar, baking powder, lemon zest and salt to combine. In a separate bowl, whisk buttermilk, oil and egg yolks to combine. Whisk into flour mixture and stir until just blended (a few lumps are okay). Whip egg whites until they hold a soft peak when beaters are lifted, and fold gently into waffle batter.

Lightly grease a preheated waffle iron and spoon about 1/3 cup (75 mL) of batter onto iron (for a 4-inch/10-cm waffle). Close and cook until steam from the waffles dies away, about 4 minutes (depending on your iron). Remove waffles and keep warm in a low (250°F/115°C) oven until ready to serve.

Waffles are best served fresh, but if preparing in advance, let waffles cool, freeze, then warm uncovered in a 300°F (150°C) oven for 20 minutes.

FOR GARNISH, whip cream to soft peaks and stir in sugar. Arrange 2 waffles on a plate and dollop cream on top. Drizzle syrup over, top with quartered strawberries and dust with icing sugar.

NOTES

✧ I find the best waffle recipes call for folding in whipped egg white right before you make them. If you want to make these in the morning, but wish to work ahead, prepare the batter except for the egg whites the evening before, and refrigerate overnight. Whip and fold in the whites right before making the waffles.

✧ No matter how much of a professional you are, the first batch of waffles never comes out pretty (just like the first pancake). Those are yours to sneak away and snack on before anyone has even woken to the smell of coffee brewing.

Butter

Second only to sugar, butter has to be my most commonly used ingredient. Nothing beats the taste of butter, and these recipes really let it shine.

Shortbread Cookies

MAKES ABOUT 3 DOZEN

1 cup	250 mL	unsalted butter, room temperature
½ cup + 2 Tbsp	150 mL	icing sugar
¼ cup	60 mL	cornstarch or rice flour
1½ cups	375 mL	all-purpose flour
½ tsp	2 mL	fine salt
1 tsp	5 mL	vanilla extract

There are so many styles of shortbread to choose from, and you probably have a recipe that has been made by generations of your family. This style is a tender, drop shortbread—different than the firmer-style shortbread that is pressed into a pan and cut into wedges.

✧ ✧ ✧

Preheat oven to 350°F (180°C). Beat butter until light and fluffy. Sift in icing sugar and beat again until fluffy, scraping down the sides of the bowl often. Sift in cornstarch or rice flour and blend in. Sift in all-purpose flour and salt and mix until dough comes together (it will be soft). Stir in vanilla.

Spoon large teaspoonfuls of cookie dough (or use a small ice cream scoop) onto an ungreased cookie sheet, leaving 2 inches (5 cm) between cookies, and bake for 18 to 20 minutes, until bottoms brown lightly. Remove from cookie sheet to cool on a rack.

Switch Up
Chocolate Nougat Shortbread

These cookies have become a staple in my holiday cookie tins. They're so popular, I have friends ask for a cookie tin just of these shortbread!

✧ ✧ ✧

Prepare shortbread recipe as on page 60. Before baking, press a triangle of chocolate nougat candy into the centre of each cookie.

NOTES

✧ I got this recipe from the owner of a lovely tea room—a great place for a girlie lunch. Going for high tea is one of my secret little indulgences. When I'm traveling, if I can sneak away to a posh hotel for tea, it's like an afternoon at the spa for me.

✧ This switch-up version with chocolate nougat is now a holiday staple for me, and shortbread is one of the things that improves as it sits in the cookie tin.

✧ Cornstarch or rice flour is the secret to these tender cookies—either works well and neither imparts a taste that interferes with that buttery goodness.

Golden Buttercream Cake

Golden Buttercream Cake

CAKE

1 cup	250 mL	unsalted butter, room temperature
2 cups	500 mL	sugar
2 tsp	10 mL	vanilla extract
4	4	large eggs, room temperature
2 3/4 cups	675 mL	pastry flour
1/2 tsp	2 mL	baking powder
1/4 tsp	1 mL	baking soda
1/2 tsp	2 mL	fine salt
1 cup	250 mL	buttermilk, room temperature

BUTTERCREAM FROSTING

1 1/2 cups	375 mL	unsalted butter, room temperature
4	4	large egg whites
1/2 tsp	2 mL	cream of tartar
3 Tbsp + 10 Tbsp	45 mL + 140 mL	sugar
1/4 cup	60 mL	water
1 1/2 tsp	7 mL	vanilla extract
pinch	pinch	fine salt

FOR CAKE, preheat oven to 325°F (160°C) and grease and flour three 9-inch (23-cm) round cake pans.

Beat butter in a mixer fitted with the paddle attachment or with electric beaters until light and fluffy. Add sugar and again beat until fluffy. Beat in vanilla and add eggs, one at a time, blending well after each addition. In a separate bowl, sift flour, baking powder, baking soda and salt. Add flour, 1/2 cup (125 mL) at a time, mixing on a lower speed and alternating with buttermilk until all has been added and batter is smooth. Divide batter evenly between the 3 prepared pans (I use a measuring cup to dole out the batter equally) and level with a spatula. Give the cake pans a gentle tap on the counter to loosen up any trapped air bubbles. Bake on centre rack of the oven for 30 to 40 minutes, rotating pans halfway through cooking, until a tester inserted in the centre of the cake comes out clean. Cool cakes for 20 minutes, then turn out on a rack to cool completely.

FOR BUTTERCREAM FROSTING, beat softened butter until fluffy and set aside. In a separate bowl whip egg whites with cream of tartar until foamy. Gradually pour in 3 Tbsp (45 mL) sugar while whipping and whip to soft peaks (the peaks will curl when whisk is lifted). Set aside.

In a small saucepan, bring remaining 10 Tbsp (140 mL) sugar and water to a boil. Continue boiling until temperature reads 239°F (115°C) (softball stage) on a candy thermometer. Remove from heat and immediately and carefully pour sugar syrup into whipped egg whites by pouring slowly down the side of the bowl while beating whites (pouring down the side of the bowl will prevent splashing). Beat whites on high speed until whites have cooled to room temperature. Once cooled, add soft butter, a little at a time, until all has been added. Continue beating until buttercream is smooth and fluffy, about 2 minutes. Beat in vanilla and salt. Buttercream frosting can be used immediately or refrigerated for up to a week. If using later, bring to room temperature and beat with an electric mixer until smooth again.

(CONTINUES NEXT PAGE)

SIMPLE SYRUP AND ASSEMBLY

½ cup	125 mL	sugar
½ cup	125 mL	water
1 tsp	5 mL	vanilla extract
¾ cup	175 mL	red currant or raspberry jam, stirred
		icing sugar, for dusting

FOR SIMPLE SYRUP, bring sugar and water to a simmer and cook until sugar is dissolved. Stir in vanilla and cool.

TO ASSEMBLE, place one cake layer on a plate and brush lightly with simple syrup (this keeps cake moist and makes spreading frosting easier). Dollop buttercream on top and spread smoothly, to about ¼ inch (5 mm) thick, pushing frosting right to the edges. Spread red currant jam over buttercream. Place second cake layer on top and repeat brushing with syrup, frosting and jam. Place final cake layer on top. Chill cake until ready to present and serve, but let sit at room temperature for 15 minutes before slicing. Dust top of cake generously with icing sugar.

NOTES

◇ Always use unsalted butter in your baking, for a number of reasons.
  1. It is fresher tasting.
  2. Recipe by recipe, salt requirements vary, so this way you control the salt.
  3. Salt content varies in different brands—use unsalted to stay on a level playing field.

◇ When you taste this rich and creamy, yet light and fluffy frosting, you will understand why it is called "buttercream."

◇ This cake is like a slightly richer version of a Victoria sponge—I find it a little easier to make, and it stays fresh a bit longer.

Citrus Zest

Citrus zest adds light, summery fragrance to desserts without introducing any tartness. Any of your favourite zests or even a blend can be used in these recipes. Grapefruit zest is the only one I watch for—in large amounts, it can impart a little too intense a bitter taste.

Lemon Pudding Cakes

SERVES 4

6 Tbsp	90 mL	unsalted butter, room temperature
2/3 cup	150 mL	demerara sugar
4	4	lemons, zest and juice
4	4	large eggs, separated
1/2 cup	125 mL	all-purpose flour
1/2 tsp	2 mL	baking powder
1/2 cup	125 mL	2% milk

Served in the ramekin they're baked in, these cakes create a lemon sauce in the bottom as they bake. Perfect for a chilly winter's evening.

◇ ◇ ◇

Preheat oven to 350°F (180°C). Butter four 6-ounce (175-mL) ramekins and place in a baking pan with a 2-inch (5-cm) lip.

Using an electric mixer, beat butter and sugar until pale and fluffy. Add lemon zest and juice and then add egg yolks, one at a time (don't worry if mixture curdles—it'll work out fine). On low speed, add in flour and baking powder, then add milk a little at a time, until mixture is evenly blended. Whip egg whites until they hold a stiff peak. Gently fold a third of the whites into the lemon mixture, then fold in the remaining two-thirds of whites. Spoon batter into prepared ramekins. Pour boiling water around the ramekins to come halfway up and bake for 35 minutes, until puddings are risen and tops are a rich golden brown. Serve warm.

NOTES

◇ Demerara sugar is the secret to the sauce in this recipe. Available at most grocery stores these days (or check out a health food store), it is heavier and denser than regular brown sugar, and pulls the juices toward the bottom as it slowly sinks while baking.

◇ I like to use a plane zester for a really fine zest, but if you like the texture of bits of zest in your baking, use a box grater or peel the outer zest off the lemon and finely chop with a knife.

◇ If using a sweeter fruit like orange, as in the Switch-Up, notice that you have to keep in a bit of the lemon for its tartness.

Orange Pudding Cakes with Citrus Cream

CITRUS CREAM

MAKES ABOUT 2 CUPS (500 mL)

1 cup	250 mL	whipping cream
3 Tbsp	45 mL	sugar
2 Tbsp	30 mL	sour cream or plain yogurt
1 tsp	5 mL	orange zest
1 tsp	5 mL	lemon zest
1 tsp	5 mL	lime zest
1 Tbsp	15 mL	lime juice

You'll find that many of your favourite citrus recipes can be re-invented just by changing the choice of citrus.

✧ ✧ ✧

Prepare the recipe as on page 65, except replace the 4 lemons with 3 oranges and 1 lemon and serve with Citrus Cream.

FOR CITRUS CREAM, whip cream to soft peaks and fold in remaining ingredients. Top each pudding cake with a dollop of Citrus Cream.

Lime Chiffon Semifreddo with Almond Toast

SERVES 8

LIME CHIFFON SEMIFREDDO

4	4	large egg whites
1 cup	250 mL	icing sugar, sifted
1½ cups	375 mL	whipping cream
½ cup	125 mL	sour cream
2 Tbsp	30 mL	fresh lime juice
2 tsp	10 mL	finely grated lime zest

ALMOND TOAST

6	6	large egg whites
pinch	pinch	fine salt
1 cup	250 mL	sugar
1¼ cups	300 mL	all-purpose flour
1 cup	250 mL	whole almonds

NOTES

❖ I make this semifreddo when I feel like showing off a bit but don't want to turn on the oven, or when I don't have a lot of time to spend in the kitchen. Just be sure to allow enough time in the freezer, and dessert is ready to go. It's perfect for a busy Saturday when I'm having guests but have to spend the day running around.

❖ The Almond Toast is truly something different—really a twice-baked meringue. It can be used just like biscotti, beside a coffee or in this case, as a garnish next to a creamy dessert.

❖ The semifreddo can also be spread into a lined loaf pan and sliced like a terrine, or scooped like ice cream, if you wish.

Translated from Italian, semifreddo means "half frozen." This dessert is a creamy, frozen mousse—really a fluffy ice cream made without using an ice cream maker.

❖ ❖ ❖

FOR SEMIFREDDO, line eight 5-ounce (150-mL) ramekins completely with plastic wrap, so that the wrap hangs over the sides. Place ramekins on a tray and freeze.

Whip egg whites until foamy. Add ¼ cup (60 mL) of the icing sugar and whip until whites hold a stiff peak. In another bowl whip cream to a soft peak. Reduce speed and add remaining ¾ cup (175 mL) icing sugar, sour cream, lime juice and lime zest. Add a large spoonful of cream to whipped whites and gently fold in. Fold whites into cream in two additions. Pour mixture into prepared ramekins, cover and freeze for at least four hours.

To serve, turn semifreddos out onto a plate and peel away plastic wrap. Serve with Almond Toast.

FOR ALMOND TOAST, preheat oven to 350°F (180°C) and line a 9- × 5-inch (2-L) loaf pan with parchment paper (do not grease). Whip whites and salt until foamy, then gradually pour in sugar. Continue whipping until whites hold a stiff peak. Fold in sifted flour, then fold in almonds. Scrape meringue into prepared pan and bake for 35 minutes, until top is richly browned. Allow to cool, then wrap and freeze overnight.

Preheat oven to 175°F (80°C) and line a baking tray with parchment. Using a serrated knife, slice thin slices of loaf, about ¼ inch (5 mm) thick or less, and place on a baking sheet. Bake until dry and crisp, but not browned, 20 to 30 minutes. Store in an airtight container until ready to serve. Almond Toasts will keep up to 2 weeks.

Tart Lemon

Like good apple recipes, everyone needs a collection of good lemon recipes in their baking repertoire. I am a big fan of lemon in winter, but when berries are in season, it's also hard to resist a lemon recipe like the ones below to complement them.

Lemon Pound Cake

MAKES ONE 9- × 5-INCH (2-L) LOAF PAN

LEMON POUND CAKE

1 2/3 cups	400 mL	pastry flour
1/2 tsp	2 mL	fine salt
1 cup	250 mL	unsalted butter, room temperature
1 1/2 cups	375 mL	sugar
5	5	large eggs, room temperature
1 1/2 tsp	7 mL	vanilla extract
1 Tbsp	15 mL	finely grated lemon zest

GLAZE

1/3 cup	75 mL	fresh lemon juice
1/2 cup	125 mL	sugar
		zest of 1 lemon, removed in thin strips

Fundamentally simple in concept, a well-made pound cake is a beautiful thing—and it should neither slice nor taste like it weighs a pound, either.

❖ ❖ ❖

Preheat oven to 325°F (160°C). Grease a 9- × 5-inch (2-L) loaf tin and dust with flour, shaking out excess.

FOR LEMON POUND CAKE, sift flour and salt twice and set aside. With an electric mixer, beat butter until creamy and light-coloured. While beating, gradually pour in sugar, then increase speed and beat until light and fluffy. In a separate bowl, whisk eggs to blend, but do not add air. Add beaten eggs in 3 additions, beating for 20 seconds after each addition. If batter looks like it is starting to curdle, wrap a warm, damp tea towel around the bowl and continue beating. Mix in vanilla and lemon zest. Fold in flour by hand in 2 additions. Spread batter into prepared pan and bake for 65 to 70 minutes, until a tester inserted in the centre of the cake comes out clean. Allow cake to cool for 15 minutes, then turn out onto a rack to cool completely.

While cake is cooling prepare glaze. Heat lemon juice, sugar and zest until sugar dissolves. While glaze and cake are still warm, poke holes in cake with a skewer and spoon glaze over cake. The syrup will soak in and set with a crunchy exterior, and the zest will rest on top.

NOTES

❖ A good pound cake should be dense, but not heavy. Using pastry flour and sifting it twice helps create a fine texture, and the large volume of eggs keeps it light as it bakes.

❖ It is very important that all ingredients are the same temperature. While I normally use the microwave to soften butter for most recipes, I do let my butter and eggs sit on the counter to come up to room temperature for this cake.

Lemon Layer Cakes

LEMON CREAM

½ cup	125 mL	whipping cream, whipped to soft peaks
¼ cup	60 mL	sour cream
¼ cup	60 mL	sugar
2 tsp	10 mL	finely grated lemon zest
2 Tbsp	30 mL	fresh lemon juice

LEMON CURD

2	2	large egg yolks
2	2	large eggs
⅓ cup	75 mL	sugar
2 Tbsp	30 mL	finely grated lemon zest
½ cup	125 mL	fresh lemon juice
½ cup	125 mL	unsalted butter at room temperature
¼ cup	60 mL	full-fat sour cream
2 Tbsp	30 mL	table cream (18%)

✧ Add all ingredients to the butter base gradually, for smooth, even incorporation—this will ensure a tender, evenly textured cake. As soon as the flour has been evenly mixed in, stop blending.

✧ My last bit of advice—beat that butter until it is very fluffy before adding sugar, and do whisk those eggs before adding them to the butter base. It's the little steps like this that make the difference.

This is a fabulous dessert to serve to lemon lovers. The tart curd and delicate cream are spectacular when layered with slices of the pound cake.

✧ ✧ ✧

Prepare the Lemon Pound Cake (page 68).

FOR LEMON CREAM, stir whipped cream, sour cream and sugar gently together. Stir in lemon zest and juice and chill until ready to serve. Lemon cream will thicken as it sets.

FOR LEMON CURD, whisk egg yolks, eggs, sugar, lemon zest and juice in a bowl over a pot of gently simmering water until thick (you should be able to spoon it, not pour it). Remove from heat and scrape into a food processor. Pulse in butter, sour cream and table cream until smooth. Scrape curd into a bowl and cover surface with plastic wrap. Chill for at least 3 hours.

To assemble, cut 12 slices of pound cake, trim crust and divide each slice into two pieces. For each serving, layer 3 pieces of cake with a dollop of lemon cream and lemon curd between the layers.

Lemon Crème Brûlée

LEMON CURD

2	2	large egg yolks
2	2	large eggs
1/3 cup	75 mL	sugar
2 Tbsp	30 mL	finely grated lemon zest
1/2 cup	125 mL	fresh lemon juice
1/2 cup	125 mL	unsalted butter at room temperature
1/4 cup	60 mL	full-fat sour cream
2 Tbsp	30 mL	table cream (18%)

CRÈME

1 1/2 cups	375 mL	whole milk
1 1/2 cups	375 mL	table cream (18%)
3	3	large eggs
3	3	large egg yolks
1/3 cup	75 mL	sugar
pinch	pinch	fine salt
1 tsp	5 mL	orange liqueur, optional

BRÛLÉE

1/2 cup	125 mL	sugar
1/4 cup	60 mL	water

NOTES

❖ The lemon curd I use in this recipe is a little different from my other recipes—I found the other versions would overcook and be absorbed into the custard. This recipe creates a hidden layer under crème brûlée for a tart surprise.

❖ It always happens that, when I pull my custards out of the oven, I accidentally splash a little water on the top of at least one. To fix this, gently set the corner of a paper towel on the water. The towel will absorb the water without damaging the top of the custard.

❖ This technique for glazing the top of the custards lasts longer than the normal torch method of brûlée. You can coat the tops of the custards up to 3 hours in advance, and they will still crack when you tap your spoon on them.

Now you can make a delicious crème brûlée without using a blowtorch or broiling it in the oven. Pouring liquid caramelized sugar over chilled brûlées coats the custards beautifully, and gives the brittle, glazed finish of a true brûlée.

❖ ❖ ❖

FOR LEMON CURD, whisk egg yolks, eggs, sugar, lemon zest and juice in a bowl over a pot of gently simmering water until thick (you should be able to spoon it, not pour it). Remove from heat and scrape into a food processor. Pulse in butter, sour cream and table cream until smooth. Scrape curd into a bowl and cover surface with plastic wrap. Chill for at least 3 hours.

FOR CRÈME, heat milk and cream in a saucepan. In a bowl, gently whisk eggs, egg yolks, sugar and salt. Ladle about 1/2 cup (125 mL) of milk mixture into eggs, whisking in. Continue adding milk and whisking until it has all been blended in. (Do not whisk too vigorously.) Stir in liqueur, if using. Strain and chill completely.

Preheat oven to 350°F (180°C). Arrange eight 6-ounce (175-mL) tempered glass dishes or ceramic ramekins on a tea towel in a baking dish with a 2-inch (5-cm) lip. Divide lemon curd evenly between ramekins and spread. Carefully pour the chilled custard over the lemon curd, dabbing off any bubbles with the edge of a paper towel. Pour boiling water around baking dishes or ramekins. Cover pan loosely with foil and bake for 35 to 40 minutes, until custards are set but centres still jiggle when tapped.

Remove from water bath, and let cool for 20 minutes, then chill completely, at least 4 hours.

FOR BRÛLÉE, place sugar and water in a saucepan over high heat and boil, without stirring, until it is a light amber colour. While cooking, occasionally brush down the sides of the pot with a clean brush dipped in water. Immerse pot in a bowl of cold water to halt cooking, then spoon a thin layer of caramel over each cooled custard, swirling cup to coat evenly.

The crème brûlées can be returned to the fridge and served up to 3 hours later.

Lemon Crème Brûlée

Bright as sunshine, orange is a visual wake-up and citrus flavours rouse our taste buds as well. Not only citrus speaks of vivacious orange — other morning-like tones and tastes, such as pineapple, speak the same tale.

You may not be able to get away with serving these desserts for break-fast, but their vibrancy does shine so brightly after sunset.

orange

JUICES | TANGERINE | ORANGE LIQUEUR

Juices

Freshly squeezed juices are certainly the tastiest to use in sweet delights, but concentrate will work in a pinch. Go for pure juice flavours, not "cocktails" that are sweetened and enhanced.

Orange Melon Soup

SERVES 6

1 Tbsp	15 mL	finely grated orange zest
½ cup	125 mL	pineapple juice
⅓ cup	75 mL	sugar
2 tsp	10 mL	freshly grated ginger
4 cups	1 L	peeled and diced cantaloupe
1 cup	250 mL	yogurt
¾ cup	175 mL	sour cream
1 tsp	5 mL	vanilla extract
1 Tbsp	15 mL	honey
2 Tbsp	30 mL	chopped fresh mint

I first learned this recipe at cooking school in Vail, Colorado, and even though I was far from home, its taste immediately brought back my childhood memories of slurping on a Creamsicle.

✧ ✧ ✧

Simmer orange zest, juice, sugar and ginger until the consistency of a thin syrup. Remove from heat and cool. In a blender, purée cantaloupe with cooled syrup until smooth. Add yogurt, ½ cup (125 mL) of the sour cream and vanilla and purée until smooth. Chill for at least 4 hours before serving.

For garnish, stir remaining ¼ cup (50 mL) sour cream with honey and mint. Dollop or swirl sweetened sour cream on soup before serving.

NOTES

✧ To select a ripe melon, press gently around the stem end—it should give just a little. Then take a quick sniff—the stem end should smell just faintly of melon if it's ripe.

✧ When looking for pineapple juice, I prefer frozen over canned for that fresher taste. It's great that so many grocery stores now offer a fruit service section, where juices are freshly squeezed and fruit salads are prepared to order.

[Switch Up]
Orange Melon Granita

Granita has to be the simplest frozen dessert to make, as it doesn't require an ice cream maker. Just because it's easy, doesn't mean it's any less delicious than a dessert made with more effort.

◇ ◇ ◇

Simply prepare Orange Melon Soup recipe (page 75) and freeze in a non-reactive container, stirring once after the first two hours, until completely frozen. To serve, scrape up granules with a fork and spoon into tall glasses. Garnish with a sprig of fresh mint.

Pineapple Upside-down Cake with Piña Colada Ice Cream

MAKES ONE 10-INCH (25-CM) CAKE
SERVES 12 TO 16

FRUIT

2 cups	500 mL	sliced pineapple (cored rounds), about 1/2 pineapple
2 Tbsp	30 mL	pineapple juice
1/4 cup	60 mL	unsalted butter
3/4 cup	175 mL	dark brown sugar, packed
1 tsp	5 mL	vanilla extract

CAKE

1/3 cup	75 mL	whipping cream
4	4	large egg whites
3	3	large egg yolks
1 tsp	5 mL	vanilla extract
1/2 tsp	2 mL	almond extract
1 1/2 cups	375 mL	all-purpose flour
3/4 cup	175 mL	sugar
1/4 cup	60 mL	cornmeal
1 tsp	5 mL	baking powder
1/4 tsp	1 mL	baking soda
1/2 tsp	2 mL	fine salt
1/3 cup	75 mL	unsalted butter, room temperature
1/3 cup	75 mL	pineapple juice

When was the last time you ate a slice of this cake? Mom may have made it years ago, but don't neglect this recipe now. I feature it at the bakery in the winter, and it's always a hit.

❖ ❖ ❖

Preheat oven to 350°F (180°C). Grease a 10-inch (25-cm) springform pan and line bottom with parchment paper. Wrap outside bottom and sides of pan with plastic and then aluminum foil—this will catch any syrup that oozes out as the cake bakes.

FOR FRUIT, toss pineapple with pineapple juice. Melt butter and brown sugar together over medium heat. Stir in fruit and vanilla and pour into prepared pan, arranging pineapple slices so they sit flat.

FOR CAKE, stir cream, egg whites, yolks and extracts to blend and set aside. In a large bowl sift flour, sugar, cornmeal, baking powder, baking soda and salt. Add butter and pineapple juice to flour and beat with electric mixers until blended. Add half of the egg mixture and blend. Add remaining egg mixture and blend until smooth, scraping the sides of the bowl often. Scrape batter over pineapple in the prepared springform pan and spread to level. Bake for 30 minutes or until a tester inserted in the centre of the cake comes out clean.

Let cake cool for 15 minutes, then invert onto a plate to cool completely. Slice and serve with Piña Colada Ice Cream (recipe follows).

NOTES

❖ This method for making a cake may seem unfamiliar to a seasoned baker. The instructions resemble a scone technique more than a cake at first, but this method really seems to work with the upside-down principle. The cake holds its own as it bakes above the sugary fruit layer, without getting at all soggy, and the taste and texture is definitely all cake—tender and sweet.

❖ I really like what that little bit of cornmeal lends to the cake. A beautiful golden colour results and the texture remains tender and moist.

Piña Colada Ice Cream

2 | 2	ripe golden pineapples (about 2 lbs/900 g)
1/4 cup | 60 mL	sugar
1 Tbsp | 15 mL	fresh lime juice
1 1/4 cups | 300 mL	whipping cream
2/3 cup | 150 mL	sweetened coconut

This ice cream is perfect on its own, or can be adapted for pool-side consumption when mixed in a blender with a little rum.

❖ ❖ ❖

Peel and core pineapples, removing eyes. Dice up 2 1/2 cups (625 mL) of pineapple and set aside. Purée remaining pineapple in a blender or food processor and stir in sugar and lime juice. Whip cream to soft peaks and fold into pineapple mixture. Stir in coconut and pour into an ice cream maker, following manufacturer's instructions. Before ice cream has completely frozen, stir in diced pineapple. Spoon into a non-reactive container and freeze for at least 2 hours before serving.

NOTES

❖ I have never been to Hawaii, but I love the coconut pineapple blend in a Pina Colada. Michael and I have sworn that we would spend our tenth wedding anniversary there. Just a few more years to go, honey...

Tangerine

Tangerines are a sweet, juicy member of the mandarin family, and their honeyed citrus juices and subtle zest lend such delicacy to sweets. Beware the seeds, though — tangerines are notorious for being seedy, which is why I prefer to zest and juice them rather than try to eat them whole.

Tangerine Cupcakes

MAKES 18 CUPCAKES

CUPCAKES

2 ¼ cups	550 mL	pastry flour
1 ½ cups	375 mL	sugar
1 Tbsp	15 mL	baking powder
1 tsp	5 mL	fine salt
⅓ cup	75 mL	canola oil
¾ cup	175 mL	buttermilk
1 ½ tsp	7 mL	vanilla extract
1 Tbsp	15 mL	freshly grated tangerine zest
¼ cup	60 mL	fresh tangerine juice
2	2	large eggs, separated

ICING

⅓ cup	75 mL	unsalted butter, room temperature
3 ½ cups	875 mL	icing sugar, sifted
1 tsp	5 mL	vanilla extract
1 Tbsp	15 mL	freshly grated tangerine zest
1 to 2 Tbsp	15 to 30 mL	fresh tangerine juice
3 Tbsp	45 mL	orange sugar sprinkles

These are such dainty, delicate cupcakes — perfect with the sophisticated addition of tangerine. A simple buttercream makes them even more heavenly.

❖ ❖ ❖

FOR CUPCAKES, preheat oven to 375° F (180°C) and line muffin tins with paper cups.

Sift flour, 1 cup (250 mL) of the sugar, baking powder and salt into a large mixing bowl. Make a well in the centre of the flour mixture and add oil, buttermilk, vanilla and tangerine zest. Beat one minute with electric mixer. Add tangerine juice and egg yolks and beat another minute. In a separate bowl and using clean beaters, whip egg whites until foamy. Gradually pour in remaining ½ cup (125 mL) sugar and whip until whites hold a stiff peak. Fold whites gently into batter and spoon into muffin cups. Bake for 15 minutes or until cupcakes spring back when pressed. Allow to cool.

FOR ICING, beat butter until fluffy. On low speed beat in icing sugar until smooth. Beat in vanilla, zest and tangerine juice. If icing is too thin, add a touch more icing sugar. Spread icing onto cupcakes, garnish with sprinkles and serve.

NOTES

❖ If tangerines aren't in season, try another member of the family, like mandarins or clementines. All have that same perfect sweetness and relatively low acidity.

❖ Cupcakes are still as popular as ever, and I am often asked to construct cupcake wedding cakes. Lovely and simple on their own, these cupcakes could be garnished with any adornment that coordinates with a shower or wedding.

Tangerine Cupcakes

[Switch Up]
Tangerine Chocolate Cupcakes

CHOCOLATE ICING

MAKES ABOUT 2 CUPS (500 ML)

¹/₃ cup	75 mL	unsalted butter, room temperature
3 cups	750 mL	icing sugar, sifted
¹/₂ cup	125 mL	cocoa, sifted
1 tsp	5 mL	vanilla
1 Tbsp	15 mL	freshly grated tangerine zest
1 to 2 Tbsp	15 to 30 mL	fresh tangerine juice
2 ounces	60 g	semisweet chocolate, melted
		orange-coloured candies, for garnish

Few things beat a good, basic buttercream on a cupcake, except maybe a chocolate one. Of course, you have to lick off the icing first, before you eat the cupcake.

✧ ✧ ✧

Prepare Tangerine Cupcakes (page 79).

FOR ICING, beat butter until fluffy. On low speed beat in icing sugar and cocoa until smooth. Beat in vanilla, zest and tangerine juice. Stir in melted chocolate. If the icing is too thin, add a touch more icing sugar. Spread icing onto cupcakes and garnish with orange-coloured candies of your choice.

Tangerine Fool Cake

CAKE

6	6	large eggs
1 cup	250 mL	sugar
1 cup	250 mL	all-purpose flour
1/2 tsp	2 mL	fine salt
1/3 cup	75 mL	unsalted butter, melted
1 tsp	5 mL	vanilla extract
2 tsp	10 mL	tangerine zest
1 Tbsp	15 mL	tangerine juice

MERINGUE

2	2	large egg whites, room temperature
1/2 tsp	2 mL	cream of tartar
1/2 cup	125 mL	sugar

FOOL

2 cups	500 mL	whipping cream
3 Tbsp	45 mL	sour cream
1/4 cup	60 mL	sugar
1 Tbsp	15 mL	coarsely grated tangerine zest
3 Tbsp	45 mL	tangerine juice

The yummy components of this dessert are assembled on the plate right before serving, and the combined effect is like a trifle. You could also ice the square tangerine cake with the "fool" and slice to serve.

❖ ❖ ❖

FOR CAKE, preheat oven to 350°F (180°C) and line an 8-inch (2-L) square pan with parchment so that it hangs over the sides (do not grease).

Whisk eggs and sugar over a pot of gently simmering water for about 3 minutes, so that the eggs are just warm to the touch. Remove from heat and whip mixture with an electric mixer or in a stand-up mixer until pale yellow, glossy and firm, about 10 minutes.

Sift flour and salt, and gently but quickly fold into eggs in two additions. Combine melted butter, vanilla, zest and juice. Stir about 1/3 cup (75 mL) of cake batter into melted butter until smooth, then stir mixture into cake batter (this will keep the butter from sinking to the bottom). Scrape batter into prepared pan and bake for 30 minutes, or until cake springs back when gently pressed. Allow cake to cool for 20 minutes, then turn out onto a cooling rack to cool completely.

FOR MERINGUE, reduce oven temperature to 250°F (120°C) and line a baking tray with parchment paper.

Whip egg whites with cream of tartar until foamy. Gradually add sugar and continue whipping until whites are glossy and hold a stiff peak. Spread meringue in an even layer onto prepared baking tray. Bake for about 40 minutes, or until dry (times may vary depending on air humidity).

FOR FOOL, whip cream to medium peaks and stir in remaining ingredients. Break meringue into pieces and fold into whipped cream.

ASSEMBLY

½ cup | 125 mL	fresh tangerine juice
2 Tbsp | 30 mL	lemon juice
½ cup | 125 mL	sugar
	tangerine slices, for garnish

TO ASSEMBLE, heat tangerine juice and lemon juice with sugar until sugar is dissolved, then remove from heat. Trim outside of cake to remove brown edges and cut into 9 squares, placing each square on a plate. Brush each square with tangerine syrup. Top each square with a generous dollop of fool and garnish with a tangerine slice. Serve immediately.

NOTES

❖ This cake is a genoise sponge, the base for many classic cakes and tortes. The trick to a nicely textured sponge is to work very quickly when you fold in the dry ingredients and butter. This will give the whipped eggs less time to deflate.

❖ Warming the eggs before whipping promotes a greater volume, and by not greasing the pan before you bake the cake, you give the batter an edge to cling to as it rises in the oven.

❖ The beauty of this dessert is in the teasing of the senses. The subtle fragrance of tangerines, the gentle hues of orange, the crunch of meringue and the unctuous taste at first bite—it will send shivers down your spine.

Orange Liqueur

There are many brands of orange liqueur—some sweet, some with a hint of bitterness. Any style will work in these recipes—just use your favourite.

Flourless Chocolate Orange Cake

8 ounces	240 g	bittersweet chocolate chopped bittersweet only
2 Tbsp	30 mL	unsalted butter
5	5	large eggs at room temperature, separated
1 tsp	5 mL	finely grated orange zest
1 cup	250 mL	ground almonds
3/4 cup + 2 Tbsp	225 mL	superfine sugar
2 Tbsp	30 mL	orange liqueur
1 tsp	5 mL	apple cider vinegar
		icing sugar and/or cocoa powder for dusting

Sinful, dense and rich, this cake is best served and stored at room temperature

❖ ❖ ❖

Preheat oven to 350°F (180°C) and grease a 10-inch (25-cm) springform pan.

Melt chocolate and butter over a pot of barely simmering water until smooth. Stir in egg yolks gently, one at a time, then fold in orange zest and ground almonds. Whip egg whites until foamy, then add sugar while whipping until whites hold a medium peak. Fold whites into chocolate mixture in 2 additions and gently fold in orange liqueur and vinegar. Pour batter into prepared pan and bake for 35 to 45 minutes, until a tester inserted in the centre of the cake comes out clean. Let cake cool completely in pan. Remove cake from pan and dust with icing sugar and/or cocoa powder.

NOTES

❖ You definitely need to use a bittersweet chocolate here. That means the cocoa content should be around 70%. This lends an intense chocolate taste to the cake.

❖ The apple cider vinegar adds an interesting element to this cake. It offsets the richness just a touch, but also prevents the top from cracking as it bakes.

[Switch Up]

Flourless Mini Chocolate Orange Cakes with Ganache   MAKES 12

CHOCOLATE ORANGE GANACHE

½ cup	125 mL	whipping cream
4 ounces	120 g	semisweet chocolate, chopped
1 Tbsp	15 mL	orange liqueur

Tarte au Chocolat is a classic French dessert filled with a rich ganache. This Switch-Up marries two great French classics together.

✧ ✧ ✧

Prepare Chocolate Orange Cake as on page 84, but spoon batter into a 12-cup muffin tin and bake at 350°F (180°C) for 18 to 20 minutes. Cool before icing.

Heat cream to just below a simmer and pour over chopped chocolate. Gently stir with a spoon until smooth. Stir in orange liqueur and set aside to cool to room temperature. Drizzle ganache on top of mini cakes.

Crêpes Suzette

CRÊPES

1 cup	250 mL	all-purpose flour
1 cup	250 mL	2% milk
1 tsp	5 mL	sugar
pinch	pinch	fine salt
3 Tbsp	45 mL	unsalted butter, melted
2	2	large eggs
1/2 cup	125 mL	beer

ORANGE BUTTER

2 Tbsp	30 mL	finely grated orange zest
1/4 cup	60 mL	sugar
3/4 cup	175 mL	unsalted butter
1/3 cup	75 mL	fresh orange juice

CRÊPES SUZETTE

2 Tbsp	30 mL	sugar
1/4 cup	60 mL	cognac
1/4 cup	60 mL	orange liqueur

NOTES

❖ It's all about the show! The crêpes and the orange butter are easy to make ahead of time, but make sure you have everything in front of you before you begin "performing." Now, with so many people having a cooking island in their kitchen, you can invite your guests to gather round as you prepare dessert in front of their very eyes.

❖ When making the crêpes in advance, be sure to store them on the counter if you're going to use them the same day, or else freeze them, even if you are making them only one day ahead. Do not refrigerate them—I find they dry out too quickly.

This is my posthumous tribute to Julia Child. I used to watch her show with fascination as she flambéed her crêpes with flourish in her beautiful oval pans. Thank you, Julia, for being one of my inspirations.

❖ ❖ ❖

FOR CRÊPES, whisk all ingredients except beer until smooth (or blend in food processor). Let batter rest for 30 minutes. Stir in beer.

Heat an 8-inch (20-cm) crêpe pan or non-stick pan over medium heat and grease lightly (you may have to play with your heat adjustments for the first few). Spoon about 2 Tbsp (30 mL) of crêpe batter into the centre of the pan and swirl to completely coat the bottom of the pan. Place back on the heat and let cook for about 2 minutes, until top of crêpe loses its shine. Flip crêpe with a spatula (or be daring and toss it in the air!) and cook 30 seconds more. Slide crêpe onto a parchment-lined baking tray and continue making crêpes until all batter is used. If preparing crêpes in advance, wrap in plastic and leave at room temperature or freeze (never in the fridge!).

FOR ORANGE BUTTER, pulse orange zest and sugar in a food processor, to extract the zest oils. Add butter and orange juice and blend until smooth. Transfer to a bowl or shape into a log and chill until firm.

FOR SUZETTE, arrange a platter with crêpes, a small bowl with the sugar, the orange butter, and the cognac and orange liqueur already measured. Have a spatula, a carving fork and a ladle at hand. It's performance time!

Place a large sauté pan over medium heat and melt orange butter—let it bubble for up to 5 minutes—it will thicken and become syrupy. Reduce heat to low and lay in a crêpe, flipping it over to coat both sides. Fold the crêpe into quarters (a carving fork works best) and move to the side. Repeat with remaining crêpes and move each crêpe to the side. Sprinkle sugar over completed crêpes. Pour cognac into the ladle and pour over crêpes. Do the same quickly with the orange liqueur. Carefully tilt the pan toward the flame (if you wish) to ignite—take care to keep back as the flames can come up quickly. With the ladle, spoon the flaming sauce over the crêpes until the flames subside, about a minute. Serve the crêpes, 2 per person and spoon sauce over.

The colour pink just sings of joy and celebration, and a wedding surely deserves a cake that reflects the happiness of the couple newly wed as well as that of their friends and family.

There are so many facets of a wedding to be planned and organized and the wedding cake may not seem as important as other key elements, but a lovely and delicious wedding cake adds to the festive feel of the day.

May the bouquet of colour in this wedding cake match the elation everyone feels as they celebrate this special day.

pink

PINK CHOCOLATE RASPBERRY FONDANT WEDDING CAKE

Pink Chocolate Raspberry Fondant Wedding Cake

Pink Chocolate Raspberry Fondant Wedding Cake

MAKES ONE 4-TIERED ROUND CAKE
SERVES 130 TO 150 PEOPLE

TOOLS REQUIRED

one 14-inch (35-cm) round cake pan,
3 inches (7.5 cm) tall

one 10-inch (25-cm) round cake pan,
3 inches (7.5cm) tall

one 8-inch (20-cm) round cake pan,
3 inches (7.5 cm) tall

one 6-inch (15-cm) round cake pan,
3 inches (7.5 cm) tall

2 cardboard cake bases, 10,
8 and 6 inches (25, 20 and 15 cm) respectively

1 cake platter, at least 16 inches
(40 cm) across

untreated wooden doweling,
3/8 inch (0.7 cm) diameter

offset spatula

piping bags and tips

cake wheel or lazy susan

GINGERED CHOCOLATE CAKE

5 cups	1.25 L	unsalted butter, room temperature
10 cups	2.5 L	sugar
5 cups	1.25 L	Dutch process cocoa powder, sifted
10	10	large eggs, room temperature
5 cups	1.25 L	2% milk, room temperature
2 tbsp	30 mL	vanilla extract
12 1/2 cups	3.125 L	all purpose flour
3 tbsp	45 mL	baking powder
2 tbsp	30 mL	ground ginger
1 tbsp	15 mL	fine salt
2 tsp	10 mL	baking soda
6 cups	1.5 L	hot brewed coffee

Chocolate is second only to lemon as the most popular wedding cake flavour these days. Accented with a little ginger to spark the palate, and layered with a little raspberry jam, this cake is full of surprises even after cutting into the delicate pink and white exterior reveals its sinfully rich centre.

If you are making this cake for a relative, a friend or even yourself, remember to allow plenty of time (which will be in short supply if you are the bride — I know from experience).

❖ ❖ ❖

FOR CAKE, preheat oven to 325°F (160°C). Grease cake pans and line bottoms and sides with parchment paper. This recipe can be made in two batches by hand or in a stand mixer, or in one batch in a very large bowl using electric beaters.

Beat butter, sugar, cocoa powder and eggs until smooth and even. Add milk and vanilla and beat well. In a separate bowl, sift flour, baking powder, ginger, salt and baking soda. Add to cocoa mixture, blending until smooth. While slowly beating, pour in hot coffee. Pour batter evenly between pans (put them side-by-side to gauge height). Bake the 6-inch (15-cm) cake for 45 to 55 minutes, until a tester inserted in the centre of the cake comes out clean. The 8-inch (20-cm) cake should take another 10 to 15 minutes, the 10-inch (25-cm) another 15 minutes more, and the 14-inch (35-cm) another 10 to 15 minutes beyond that. Let cakes cool for 20 minutes, then turn out onto cooling racks to cool completely.

VANILLA BUTTERCREAM

12 | 12	large egg whites
1/2 tsp | 2 mL	cream of tartar
pinch | pinch	fine salt
2 1/2 cups | 625 mL	sugar
1 1/2 cups | 375 mL	water
4 1/2 cups | 1.125 L	unsalted butter, room temperature
2 tsp | 10 mL	vanilla extract

ROYAL ICING

2 Tbsp | 30 mL	meringue powder
1/2 cup | 125 mL	warm water
4 1/2 cups | 1.125 L	icing sugar, sifted

FOR ASSEMBLY

2 cups | 500 mL	raspberry jam
4 1/2 lbs | 2 kg	rolling fondant
	pink paste food colouring
	egg white for attaching decorations
	pink ribbon

FOR BUTTERCREAM. This recipe can be made in two batches in a stand mixer, or in one batch in a very large bowl with electric beaters. Whip egg whites with cream of tartar and salt until foamy and add 1 cup (250 mL) of the sugar, whipping until whites hold a soft peak. In a saucepan, combine remaining 1 1/2 cups (375 mL) sugar and water and bring up to a boil. Using a candy thermometer, boil sugar without stirring until temperature reaches 240°F (115°C). If you don't have a candy thermometer, spoon a little hot sugar into a cup of cold water — if the sugar makes a "soft ball" when rolled then it's ready. Remove from heat and carefully pour the sugar down the sides of the bowl with egg whites while whipping on medium speed. Continue whipping until all sugar has been added and keep whipping until whites have cooled to room temperature, about 5 minutes. Still beating, add butter, a little at a time, until all has been added. The egg whites will deflate somewhat, but the butter adds back volume. Beat buttercream until smooth and stir in vanilla. Store buttercream at room temperature if frosting cake the same day, or refrigerate or freeze, then bring up to room temperature and beat again to return to spreadable consistency.

NOTES—CAKE & ICING

❖ It's best to make the cake a full day before you intend to ice it. It will be easier to slice the layers and fewer crumbs will come up when icing. I recommend making the cake ahead of time, wrapping well in plastic wrap and foil and freezing. Just thaw at room temperature before icing. Do not refrigerate the cake layers without icing—they will dry out.

❖ To slice level layers, place the cake on a cake board on a lazy susan or cake wheel. With a serrated knife, slice the cake from the outside toward the centre, only an inch in at a time as you turn the wheel. This will ensure that by the time you reach the centre your layers are level. Use a second cake board to lift the cut layer without cracking.

❖ This icing recipe is called an Italian buttercream and is smooth, rich, tasty and easy to work with. It adds flavour to balance the fondant, which is essentially all sugar (but it sure looks great!)

❖ An offset spatula is an indispensable tool for masking (icing) cakes. Start by putting generous amounts of icing on the top of the cake and with smooth movements, spread the icing from the centre out to the edges, so the icing hangs over. Then spread icing around the sides, connecting with the icing that is hanging over, creating a nice, clean edge. It is easier to level the cake by pulling off excess icing than trying to add more.

FOR ROYAL ICING, stir meringue powder, water and icing sugar to blend, then beat with electric mixer on high speed until mixture is stiff, about 7 minutes. Tint icing as desired. Cover surface of icing directly with plastic wrap and store at room temperature until ready to use.

TO ASSEMBLE CAKE, place 14-inch (35-cm) cake on the platter. Slice cake horizontally into 2 layers. Spread a thin coating of buttercream over bottom layer, then spread a layer of stirred raspberry jam over buttercream. Top with second cake layer. Spread an even coating of buttercream over top and sides of cake, using the frosting to even out any uneven areas and to create clean edges. Chill iced cake until ready to decorate.

Repeat slicing, filling and icing the other 3 tiers, each on a cardboard base of corresponding size. Brush away any excess crumbs and clean your work area before starting the rolling fondant.

NOTES — FONDANT

❖ A clean work area and rolling pin are essential, as fondant will pick up any crumbs as you roll.

❖ Rolling fondant is an icing that is very pliable and is easier to roll than pastry dough. If you are not happy with the shape you have achieved, just roll up the fondant and start again.

❖ I keep a tape measure nearby when rolling—I measure the diameter of the side of the cake plus the lengths of two sides so I know the diameter of the fondant needed to cover the cake entirely.

❖ Massaging the fondant gently with the palm of your hand after the cake is covered reveals any air pockets that might appear. Re-visit the cake an hour or two after covering, just to see if any new ones pop up. They can be pierced with a pin and rubbed down before the fondant sets.

❖ If you don't have a beautiful cake platter to set the cake on, consider putting the cake on a cardboard base and covering the cake AND board with fondant. A ribbon wrapped around the covered board will make it look as if it's part of the cake.

TO TINT FONDANT, add a little of the colour paste to a small ball (about ½ cup/125 mL) of fondant and knead well. Add this ball to a larger portion of fondant (about 1½ lbs/700 g) for the 10-inch (25-cm) and 6-inch (15-cm) tiers and knead by hand or in a mixer fitted with the paddle attachment (don't use electric beaters). Adjust colour as needed by adding more colour to intensify the tone, or more fondant to lighten the tone.

Lightly dust your rolling surface with icing sugar and cut off about 1½ lbs/700 g of white fondant (I like to cover the white tiers first), and roll out a circle ¼ inch (5 mm) thick and 21 inches (52 cm) in diameter. Keep remaining fondant covered at all times. Use your rolling pin to roll up fondant and lift it gently over the 14-inch (35-cm) tier. Unroll fondant over cake and gently use your hands to adhere fondant to buttercream. Trim fondant from base of cake and rub surface of fondant in a circular direction to create a smooth surface. If any air pockets appear, use a pin to release the air and rub the spot gently with your finger to erase the hole. Repeat this process with the 8-inch (20-cm) tier.

Roll the pink fondant similarly and cover the 10-inch (25-cm) and 6-inch (15-cm) tiers of cake. Let fondant set and dry overnight. Fondant can be re-rolled as many times as needed, providing that the icing does not pick up any crumbs, and reused for decoration cutouts. Now that the cakes have been covered, they are essentially protected from air and can stay fresh for 1 to 2 days.

NOTES — TIERS & DÉCOR

❖ I find five doweling pieces are necessary to build a stable and evenly supported tier as you stack the cake. Keep an eye on the tiers as you stack them—every tier has a "sweet spot," a side that looks best and should face front. Line them all up, and the front of your cake has been decided.

❖ Relax and take your time with décor. Put on your favourite CD (I actually like dance music while I'm decorating—the steady rhythm keeps my hand steady). Remember, mistakes are erasable. A misplaced dot of icing can be pulled off with a gentle stroke of the finger. Wipe the area with a dry cloth (not wet) if any colour remains. If colour is still there, rub a little icing sugar over the colour mark, and dust away—it'll be good as new.

❖ I like to practise my piping pattern on a scrap of parchment before I work on the cake, just to make sure I'm happy with my technique. I also draw a sketch of the cake, so I can see that everything is in proportion.

❖ Remember to inform your caterer or reception staff of any non-edible garnishes to the cake. Ribbons and doweling should be removed before the cake is served.

TO STACK TIERS, they must be stabilized with wooden doweling. Insert a length of doweling into base tier, at least 4 inches (10 cm) from the outside edge. Mark on the doweling where the cake reaches and remove. Cut doweling at that mark and cut 4 more identical in length (this ensures the cake will sit level). Insert the dowelling into cake in a circle and gently place 10-inch (25-cm) tier on top. Repeat this step with 8-inch (20-cm) tier and gently rest 6-inch (15-cm) tier on top.

TO DECORATE CAKE, start with the bottom tier. Wrap ribbon around base of cake. Fill a piping bag fitted with a small plain tip with pink royal icing. Pipe small dots around cake. Repeat this with the 8-inch (20-cm) tier, wrapping with ribbon and creating a different dot pattern.

For pink tiers, roll out white fondant to ¼ inch (5 mm) thickness and cut out desired shapes. Fasten décor to cake by brushing back of cutout with egg white and adhering.

Fuschia, red, blue, violet—this rainbow of colours adds sparkle and freshness and makes for very sweet endings indeed. Dewy raspberries and blueberries topping a simple mini tart is a vision of beauty, while a mix of tropical fruits sing harmoniously on a Hawaiian tart. Even humble strawberry jam adds a vibrant note to lemon scones.

Colour is definitely in fashion.

rainbow

FIGS | JAM | TROPICAL FRUIT
SUMMER FRUITS | BUMBLEBERRY | FRESH BERRIES

Figs

Fresh or dried, figs make for a sophisticated ending to a lovely meal. Dried figs may be more commonly found (and definitely not a rainbow hue), but relish the brief moments when sensually toned fresh figs are in season.

Fig Olsons

MAKES ABOUT 36 COOKIES

These cookies look just like Fig Newtons, but are simple both in their ingredient list and in their preparation.

❖ ❖ ❖

FOR DOUGH, combine flour, sugar, baking powder, baking soda, cinnamon and salt. Cut in butter until dough is a rough, crumbly texture. Add whole egg and egg yolk and blend in until dough comes together. Shape into a disk, wrap and chill for an hour.

FOR FILLING, combine all ingredients in a small saucepan and bring up to a simmer. Simmer until all liquid is absorbed, about 10 minutes. Let cool, purée in a food processor and chill completely.

Preheat oven to 375°F (190°C). On a lightly floured surface, roll out dough into a rectangle, just under ¼ inch (5 mm) thick. Using a knife or pastry cutter, cut strips of dough that are at least 4½ inches (11 cm) wide. Spoon filling (or pipe with a piping bag) along centre of strip. Brush left side of pastry dough with egg wash. Fold right side of pastry over filling, and then fold left side over so egg adheres pastry. Trim ends. Lift filled cookie tube to a parchment-lined baking sheet and press, seam-side down, to flatten. Repeat with remaining strips. Brush tops of strips with egg wash. Bake for 15 to 18 minutes, until a light golden brown. Allow to cool, then cut strips into 1-inch (2.5-cm) bites.

DOUGH

1¼ cups | 300 mL	all-purpose flour
¼ cup | 60 mL	sugar
½ tsp | 2 mL	baking powder
¼ tsp | 1 mL	baking soda
¼ tsp | 1 mL	ground cinnamon
¼ tsp | 1 mL	fine salt
½ cup | 125 mL	unsalted butter, cut into pieces and chilled
1 | 1	large egg
1 | 1	large egg yolk

FILLING

1 cup | 250 mL	diced dried figs
½ cup | 125 mL	fresh orange juice
½ cup | 125 mL	unsweetened applesauce
4 tsp | 20 mL	lemon juice
½ tsp | 2 mL	ground cinnamon
	1 egg mixed with 2 Tbsp (30 mL) water for egg wash

NOTES

❖ This recipe has very little refined sugar. The combination of dried figs, orange juice and applesauce is plenty sweet, without being cloying.

❖ Cut these cookies into bar-sized lengths for your own version of a breakfast bar—great for on the road or on the way to school.

[Switch Up]

Fig Olsons with Moroccan Mint Tea

MOROCCAN MINT TEA

2 cups | 500 mL	loosely packed fresh mint leaves
¼ cup | 60 mL	sugar
2 Tbsp | 30 mL	honey
2 Tbsp | 30 mL	loose green tea leaves
6 cups | 1.5 L	boiling water
	mint sprigs, for garnish

SERVES 6

Playing on the Mediterranean taste of figs, a mint tea is a perfect and refreshing accompaniment.

✧ ✧ ✧

Combine mint, sugar, honey and tea in a teapot. Pour boiling water over and let steep 5 to 8 minutes. Strain out mint and tea leaves and pour into glasses. Garnish with a mint sprig and serve with Fig Olsons (page 99) .

Fresh Fig and Honey Tarts

CRUST

1 cup | 250 mL	unsalted butter, room temperature
1/3 cup | 75 mL	sugar
4 | 4	large egg yolks
1/2 tsp | 2 mL	pure almond extract
2 cups | 500 mL	all-purpose flour
1 tsp | 5 mL	fine salt

CUSTARD

1 cup | 250 mL	almond milk
1/2 cup | 125 mL	whipping cream
1 | 1	vanilla bean
7 Tbsp | 105 mL	sugar
2 Tbsp | 30 mL	cornstarch
1 1/2 Tbsp | 22 mL	honey
1 | 1	large egg
1 | 1	large egg yolk

FRUIT

6 | 6	fresh figs
1 1/2 cups | 375 mL	fresh raspberries
	icing sugar, for dusting

NOTES

✧ For the pastry cream, if almond milk is not available (it is usually found at health food stores), simply use 2% milk and adjust the almond extract to taste.

✧ Fresh figs are low in acidity, so by pairing them with slightly tangy raspberries, you wake up the flavours of both fruits.

✧ Fresh figs are divine served quartered alongside a number of cheeses—try creamy fresh mascarpone, rich brie or a fruity blue.

A silky almond pastry cream hides under fresh figs and raspberries, all within a tempting sugar pastry crust. Serve these tarts after an elegant Italian supper.

✧ ✧ ✧

FOR CRUST, cream butter and sugar together until smooth. Add egg yolks and almond extract and blend. Stir in flour and salt and mix just until dough comes together. Turn out onto a lightly floured surface and knead 1 minute. Shape dough into a disk, wrap and chill for at least an hour. If making dough far in advance, remove dough from refrigerator an hour before rolling.

On a lightly floured surface, knead dough again for 1 minute. Divide dough into 6 pieces and roll out pastry to 1/4 inch (5 mm) thick. Line six 4-inch (10-cm) removable-bottom tart pans with the dough, trim rough edges and chill for 30 minutes.

Preheat oven to 375°F (190°C). Prick crust bottom with a fork and bake for 15 to 20 minutes, until edges are lightly browned and centre of shell is dry. Allow to cool before filling.

FOR CUSTARD, heat almond milk, whipping cream and seeds scraped from vanilla bean to just below a simmer. In a bowl, whisk sugar, cornstarch, honey, egg and egg yolk to blend. Gradually add heated milk to egg mixture, whisking constantly until all milk has been added. Return milk to pot and stir with a heatproof spatula or wooden spoon over medium heat until it thickens, about 4 minutes. Remove from heat and scrape immediately into a bowl. Cover surface of custard with plastic and cool completely. Once cooled, whisk custard and spoon into cooled tart shells, spreading evenly.

FOR FRUIT, cut washed figs into sixths and arrange segments in each tart, pressing fruit into custard. Repeat with raspberries. Chill until ready to serve, and dust generously with icing sugar immediately before serving.

Classic Strawberry Jam

Jam

Jam represents a rainbow of colours, and it provides a taste of each fruit as it comes into season throughout the summer months. I try and make a habit of buying fresh fruit at its peak and "putting it up" for the winter. These days, preserving is done less from necessity, and more for the pleasure in the task itself and the taste of summer that is revealed when you open a jar in early January.

Classic Strawberry Jam

3 lb | 1.5 kg	fresh strawberries (about 9 cups/2.25 L), washed and hulled
4 cups | 1 L	sugar
1/3 cup | 75 mL	lemon juice
1 Tbsp | 15 mL	unsalted butter (optional)

A good strawberry jam is straightforward and simple. While I enjoy adding bits of spice and flavouring to many sweets, I like my jam to be pure and simple.

❖ ❖ ❖

In a large saucepan, bring strawberries to a simmer over medium-low heat, mashing roughly with a potato masher or flat spoon. Add sugar and lemon juice, stir, and simmer for 2 minutes. Add butter (if using) and bring to a vigorous boil. Cook for 10 to 20 minutes, stirring often and periodically measuring the viscosity of the jam by dabbing a spoonful onto a plate and tipping the plate. Once the jam slowly drips down the plate (it should no longer run like a syrup), remove from heat and skim off foam. Fill jars following manufacturer's instructions and store in a cool, dry place away from light for up to a year.

NOTES

❖ Roughly mashing the strawberries extracts the natural pectins within the fruit, contained mostly in the seeds. Fresh fruits contain more pectin than frozen, so fresher is better here.

❖ It may be tempting to reduce the amount of sugar in this recipe, but outside of the obvious flavour change, the sugar works with the fruit pectin to "set" the jam. A reduction in the amount of sugar will result in more of a strawberry sauce than a jam.

❖ If you don't wish to jar your jams, just pack the jam into resealable plastic containers, mark the date and freeze it.

[Switch Up]

Classic Strawberry Jam with Lemon Scones   MAKES 8 TO 12 SCONES

LEMON SCONES

3 cups | 750 mL	all-purpose flour
⅓ cup | 75 mL	sugar
1 Tbsp | 15 mL	baking powder
1 Tbsp | 15 mL	lemon zest
½ tsp | 2 mL	fine salt
¾ cup | 175 mL	unsalted butter, cut into pieces and chilled
1 cup | 250 mL	half-and-half cream
1 tsp | 5 mL	vanilla extract

A great jam needs a companion, and these cream scones make a perfect mate.

❖ ❖ ❖

Preheat oven to 375°F (190°C). Place all dry ingredients in a mixing bowl, or in the bowl of an electric mixer fitted with the paddle attachment. Cut butter into dry ingredients until it resembles coarse meal. Stir together ¾ cup (175 mL) of the cream and vanilla and add to dough. Mix just until dough comes together.

Turn dough onto a lightly floured surface. Roll dough twice to an inch (2.5 cm) thickness, each time folding in half (this is the secret to a flaky scone). Roll dough to ¾ inch (2 cm) thickness and cut desired shapes. Place on a greased or parchment-lined baking sheet and brush with remaining cream. Bake for 15 to 18 minutes, until tops are nicely browned.

Apricot Marmalade Cake

APRICOT MARMALADE

2 lb	900 g	pitted fresh apricots
8 cups	2 L	sugar
1/3 cup	75 mL	fresh lemon juice
1 Tbsp	15 mL	orange zest
3/4 cup	175 mL	diced candied citrus peel
1 pouch	1 pouch	liquid pectin

APRICOT MARMALADE CAKE

1/4 cup	60 mL	demerara sugar
12 to 14	12 to 14	fresh apricots, pitted
1 cup	250 mL	unsalted butter, room temperature, plus extra for buttering
1 cup	250 mL	golden brown sugar, packed
6 Tbsp	90 mL	apricot marmalade, plus extra for brushing
4	4	large eggs
2 Tbsp	30 mL	finely grated orange zest
1/3 cup	75 mL	orange juice
1 2/3 cups	400 mL	all-purpose flour
1/2 cup	125 mL	ground almonds
1/2 tsp	2 mL	baking powder
1/4 tsp	1 mL	fine salt

This is a two-part recipe: a lovely golden apricot marmalade, and a gooey upside-down cake made using the preserve and fresh apricots. A great dessert that embraces summer.

❖ ❖ ❖

FOR APRICOT MARMALADE, bring apricots, sugar, lemon juice and orange zest to a simmer, stirring often. Purée roughly (to keep some apricot pieces intact) and return to a simmer. Stir in candied peel and pectin. Remove from heat and process according to manufacturer's instructions, or pack in containers and refrigerate.

Once opened, marmalade will keep refrigerated up to 4 months.

FOR CAKE, preheat oven to 350°F (180°C). Butter a 10-inch (25-cm) springform pan and sprinkle bottom and sides with demerara sugar. Arrange apricot halves close together in bottom of pan, flat side down.

Beat butter and brown sugar together until fluffy. Stir in marmalade and add eggs one at a time, beating well after each addition. Stir in orange zest and juice. In a separate bowl, combine flour, ground almonds, baking powder and salt and add to marmalade mixture. Stir just until blended and spread over apricots in pan. Bake for 30 to 40 minutes, until a tester inserted in the centre of the cake comes out clean.

Let cake cool for 15 minutes, then turn out onto a plate, so that apricots are on top. Brush with a little stirred apricot marmalade to add a little shine. Serve cake warm or at room temperature.

NOTES

❖ A traditional orange marmalade can sometimes take a week or more to set. This apricot marmalade, though, should set within a day.

❖ I like this marmalade recipe because I do love apricots and while I enjoy citrus desserts, I don't like tons of candied peel. This is a perfect balance for me.

❖ Using the marmalade within the body of the cake adds a fruity element and adds moisture as well. Try making these in muffin cups or ramekins for individual tea cakes.

Tropical Fruit

Tropical fruits are at their peak when we in Canada are starving for a little sunshine. Embrace pineapples, mangoes, passion fruits and even blood oranges in those winter months, or perhaps let yourself be inspired by a fortunate trip down south.

Tropical Fruit Slush

SERVES 6

½ cup | 125 mL	sugar
½ cup | 125 mL	water
1 cup | 250 mL	guava or passion fruit nectar (available at fine food, Asian or Caribbean food stores)
1 cup | 250 mL	mango nectar
2 Tbsp | 30 mL	lime juice
1 cup | 250 mL	diced fresh pineapple
1 cup | 250 mL	diced fresh papaya
	pineapple slices and mint to garnish

A fruit-laden treat like this is a refreshing finish to a spicy Indian or Thai supper.

❖ ❖ ❖

Bring sugar and water to a simmer and cook just until sugar dissolves. Chill completely.

Stir guava or passion fruit nectar, mango nectar and lime juice into sugar syrup. Purée diced pineapple and papaya and add to juice mixture. Pour into a non-reactive container, cover and freeze for one hour. Stir once or twice. Depending on your freezer, it can take from 3 to 5 hours to freeze to slush consistency. Spoon into cocktail glasses and garnish with pineapple and mint.

Another serving option is to freeze the slush completely (this is essentially a granita) and scrape granules into a glass or pulse in a blender or food processor to soften up the ice.

NOTES

❖ I prefer using a blender for this task, instead of a food processor—you get a smoother texture, so you don't have to strain out the strings of pineapple.

❖ Passion fruit is so fragrant, both as a fruit and a nectar. It's worth shopping around for. If you find a tropical fruit juice blend that includes passion fruit, that will do just fine here.

❖ Are you serving this to grownups? Sneak in a splash of that rum you brought back from the Caribbean!

Switch Up
Tropical Fruitsicles

A great treat for on the run, say, in the backyard while running under the sprinkler.

❖ ❖ ❖

Prepare recipe as on page 106 and pour into a Popsicle mould or plastic cups covered with plastic wrap with sticks inserted in the centre of each. Freeze until firm, about 6 hours.

To remove from moulds, run under cool water and then remove.

Hawaiian Tart

CRUST

2 | 2	large egg whites
½ cup | 125 mL	sugar
½ tsp | 2 mL	vanilla extract
2 cups | 500 mL	unsweetened coconut, medium shred

MOUSSE

1 cup | 250 mL	mascarpone cheese
½ cup | 125 mL	sugar
1 tsp | 5 mL	lime zest
3 Tbsp | 45 mL	fresh lime juice
½ cup | 125 mL	mango pulp (about ½ large mango)

GARNISH

1 | 1	ripe passion fruit, pulp scooped out and reserved
1 | 1	mango, sliced
1 | 1	star fruit, sliced
1 | 1	kiwi, peeled and sliced
¼ | ¼	dragonfruit, peeled and cut into slender wedges
1 | 1	small papaya, peeled and sliced

This tart has a macaroon crust filled with a mango cream and is topped by a rainbow of tropical fruits. The varied shapes and sizes of the fruits add a lot of visual appeal.

❖ ❖ ❖

FOR CRUST, preheat oven to 275°F (140°C). Stir together egg whites, sugar and vanilla until sugar has half dissolved. Stir in coconut until evenly coated with egg mixture. Grease a 10- × 4-inch (25- × 10-cm) rectangular tart tin and spoon coconut mixture into it. Press filling into pan, pressing into bottom and up sides of pan (dip your fingers in cool water while doing this to prevent the mixture from sticking to your fingers). Bake for 35 to 45 minutes, rotating pan halfway through baking. Shell should be a rich golden brown around edges. Allow to cool in pan, then remove.

FOR MOUSSE, cream mascarpone gently with sugar to soften. Add lime zest and juice and mango pulp and stir until evenly blended (switch to a whisk if you wish, but be careful not to overbeat). If mousse is too soft, chill for 20 minutes to firm up. Pipe or spoon mousse into coconut tart shell and chill until ready to serve.

GARNISH with a selection of tropical fruits immediately before serving. The tropical fruits can be sliced ahead of time, and stored under a damp cloth until ready to garnish.

NOTES

Here are some quick tips for buying and using these tropical fruits.

PASSION FRUIT – When ripe, the golf-ball-sized fruit will look purple-brown and shriveled. Cut in half to reveal the fragrant luscious fruit. Scoop out the seeds and juices and sprinkle on the dessert.

MANGO – Readily available, mangoes can be purchased green and ripened on your kitchen counter. Peel the fruits and slice into sections – just watch for the large, almond-shaped pit in the centre.

STAR FRUIT – The edges of starfruit will be just a little browned when ripe. Slice into "stars" and use immediately after slicing – the fruit will brown quickly.

KIWI – Some people eat the entire kiwi fruit, fuzzy skin and all, but I prefer to peel kiwis with a vegetable peeler. They bruise easily, so handle them gently.

DRAGONFRUIT – The dramatic dragon-like pink exterior of this fruit is cut open to reveal a pristine white flesh dotted with seeds that look like poppyseeds. Dragonfruit looks most dramatic when served with the skin on, but only the white interior (and seeds) can be eaten.

PAPAYA – Low in acidity, papayas add a subtle peach hue and nice sweetness to a tropical fruit blend. Peel, scrape out the seeds and use the fruit, although my sister-in-law, Barbara, makes a fabulous dressing by blending the seeds with vinaigrette ingredients and slicing the fruit over her salad.

Summer Fruits

It is rare that only one fruit at a time is in season during the summertime. After the fruit season officially begins with strawberries, I love that cavalcade of fruits that brings cherries, plums, apricots and peaches overlapping each other. Pick your favourite combination and bake away.

Summer Fruit Slump

SERVES 6

FRUIT

1 cup	250 mL	peeled and sliced peaches
1 cup	250 mL	sliced plums
1 cup	250 mL	sliced apricots
1 cup	250 mL	raspberries
3/4 cup	175 mL	sugar
1 Tbsp	15 mL	fresh lime juice
1 tsp	5 mL	finely grated lime zest

SLUMP

1 cup	250 mL	all-purpose flour
1/4 cup	60 mL	sugar
1/4 cup	60 mL	unsweetened coconut
1 1/2 tsp	7 mL	finely grated lime zest
1 1/2 tsp	7 mL	baking powder
1/4 tsp	1 mL	fine salt
3/4 cup	175 mL	2% milk
1	1	large egg, separated
2 Tbsp	30 mL	unsalted butter, melted

A slump looks exactly as it sounds—the soft, sweet topping melts over the fruits as it bakes, creating a cross between a cake and a cobbler.

✧ ✧ ✧

Preheat oven to 375°F (190°C).

FOR FRUIT, toss all ingredients together and spoon into a 6-cup (1.5-L) baking dish.

FOR SLUMP, stir flour, sugar, coconut, lime zest, baking powder and salt together. Whisk milk, egg yolk and melted butter, and stir into flour until combined, but not necessarily smooth (like pancake batter, a few lumps are okay). Whip egg white until it holds a medium peak (whipped white has a slight bend when whisk is lifted) and fold into batter. Spoon batter over fruit, leaving gaps for fruit juices to cook through. Bake for 20 to 25 minutes, until slump has browned and fruits are bubbling. Allow to cool for at least 15 minutes before serving.

NOTES

✧ I like what the lime juice and zest add to this recipe—it's a little more fragrant than lemon juice and really makes the sweetness of those fruits punch out.

✧ Make sure to leave gaps when spooning the slump batter onto the fruit. It will expand as it bakes, and you want to leave room for the fruit juices to bubble up.

[Switch Up]
Summer Fruit Slump with Meringue   MAKES 6 INDIVIDUAL SLUMPS

A baked meringue layer on top of the slump adds a little crunch and sweetness to an already perfect summer dessert.

❖ ❖ ❖

Preheat oven and prepare fruit as in Summer Fruit Slump (page 110). Spoon into six 1-cup (250-mL) baking dishes.

FOR SLUMP, make as above, but do not fold egg white into batter. Spoon batter over fruit, leaving gaps for fruit juices to cook through. Whip egg white until foamy then whisk in 2 Tbsp (30 mL) sugar and continue whipping until white holds a stiff peak. Spread over slumps and bake for 20 to 25 minutes, until slumps have browned and fruits are bubbling. Allow to cool for at least 15 minutes before serving.

Summer Fruit Tart

CRUST

2/3 cup | 150 mL	unsalted butter at room temperature
1 cup | 250 mL	icing sugar, sifted
1 tsp | 5 mL	finely grated lemon zest
3 | 3	large egg yolks
1 1/4 cups | 300 mL	pastry flour
1/4 tsp | 1 mL	fine salt

FILLING

2/3 cup | 150 mL	puréed raspberries, strained
3 Tbsp | 45 mL	lemon juice
6 | 6	large eggs
2 | 2	large egg yolks
1 cup | 250 mL	sugar
1 cup | 250 mL	unsalted butter, cut into pieces
2 tsp | 10 mL	lemon zest

This tart has a finely textured crust filled with a raspberry fruit curd and topped with summer's finest fruits. Perfect after a dinner al fresco.

✧ ✧ ✧

FOR CRUST, beat butter until smooth. Add icing sugar and lemon zest and cream together. Stir in egg yolks, one at a time, stirring well after each addition. Sift pastry flour and salt into butter mixture and stir just until dough comes together (turn out onto a table and bring together with your hands, if needed). Shape dough into a disk and chill for at least 1 hour.

On a lightly floured surface, roll out pastry to 1/4 inch (5 mm) thick. Sprinkle a 9-inch (23-cm) removable-bottom tart pan with a little flour and line with pastry. Trim edges and press pastry up, so it stands about 1/4 inch (5 mm) higher than the sides of the pan. Prick pastry with a fork and chill 20 minutes.

Preheat oven to 350°F (180°C). Bake pastry shell for 18 to 20 minutes, until edges are a light golden brown and centre appears dry. Allow to cool.

FOR FILLING, whisk together 1/3 cup (75 mL) of the puréed raspberries, lemon juice, eggs, yolks, and sugar. Whisk in butter and add lemon zest. Place bowl over a pot of simmering water and whisk steadily, but gently, until curd becomes thick and pale and creamy, 10 to 15 minutes. Remove from heat and cool to room temperature. Stir in remaining 1/3 cup (75 mL) puréed raspberries and pour into cooled pastry shell.

FRUIT

3 | 3	peaches or nectarines
3 | 3	apricots
1 Tbsp | 15 mL	lemon juice
1 cup | 250 mL	strawberries, hulled
1 cup | 250 mL	raspberries
1 cup | 250 mL	blueberries
1 cup | 250 mL	seasonal fruit of your choice

FOR FRUIT, slice peaches or nectarines and apricots and toss in lemon juice to prevent discolouration. Slice strawberries in half. Arrange fruit on chilled tart up to 2 hours before serving and chill until ready to serve.

NOTES

❀ Notice that half of the puréed raspberries are stirred in after the fruit curd has cooled, to bring back the colour. Raspberries lose their punchy red colour when cooked.

❀ Whenever I go to the farmers' market in the summer, I always buy far too much. I'll first walk past the berry stand and have to buy a pint of each type of berry, then I stroll past the peach stand, and mmmm…the plums and apricots look too good to pass up. You know you have to buy it now, because the season is just so fleeting.

❀ Tossing the peaches and apricots in lemon juice will help prevent them from discolouring for a few hours, but for a longer holding time, you can brush the top of the completed tart with melted clear apple jelly.

Bumbleberry

Ah, what is the mysterious bumbleberry? A rare, hard-to-find fruit that has only a brief season? Hardly.

Bumbleberry can be whatever you want it to be — it's your favourite blend of berries: strawberries, raspberries, blueberries, blackberries, mixed in any combination or quantity.

Bumbleberry Bundt Cake

MAKES ONE 12-CUP (3-L) BUNDT CAKE
SERVES 24

CAKE

³/₄ cup | 175 mL	unsalted butter, room temperature
1²/₃ cup | 400 mL	sugar
2 Tbsp | 30 mL	finely grated lemon zest
1¹/₂ Tbsp | 22 mL	vanilla extract
3 | 3	large eggs, room temperature
2 cups | 500 mL + 2 Tbsp | + 30 mL	all-purpose flour
1 cup | 250 mL	pastry flour
1 Tbsp | 15 mL	baking powder
1 tsp | 5 mL	fine salt
³/₄ cup | 175 mL	buttermilk
²/₃ cup | 150 mL	frozen raspberries
²/₃ cup | 150 mL	frozen blueberries
²/₃ cup | 150 mL	frozen blackberries

GLAZE

¹/₃ cup | 75 mL	fresh lemon juice
¹/₂ cup | 125 mL	sugar

This is a great, pound-cake-style bundt cake, absolutely loaded with a mix of berries.

◇ ◇ ◇

FOR CAKE, preheat oven to 350°F (180°C) and grease and flour a 12-cup (3-L) bundt pan. In a large bowl, cream butter and sugar until smooth. Stir in lemon zest and vanilla extract. Beat in eggs, one at a time, until fully incorporated. In separate bowl, sift 2 cups (500 mL) all-purpose flour, pastry flour, baking powder and salt. Add flour to butter mixture alternately with buttermilk, starting and finishing with the flour. Be sure to scrape the sides of the bowl often, for an evenly textured pound cake. Toss berries with remaining 2 Tbsp (30 mL) flour and fold gently into cake batter. Scrape batter into prepared pan and spread to level. Bake on centre rack of the oven for 60 to 70 minutes, until a tester inserted in the centre of the cake comes out clean.

FOR GLAZE, stir lemon juice and sugar in a small saucepan over medium heat until sugar is dissolved. As soon as cake comes out of the oven, pierce holes in it with a skewer and brush with half of the syrup. Allow cake to cool for 20 minutes, then turn it out onto a plate. Poke top of cake with more holes and brush with remaining syrup. Allow to cool before slicing.

[Switch Up]

Mini Bumbleberry Bundts with White Chocolate

There are so many lovely bundt cake moulds, both full-sized and miniature. Start a bundt pan collection, like I have!

❖ ❖ ❖

For a spectacular individual dessert presentation, prepare the Bumbleberry Bundt recipe (page 114) in 12 greased mini bundt tins. Bake for 35 to 45 minutes, until a tester inserted in the centre of the cake comes out clean. Follow the instructions for glazing the mini cakes, then dip the tops of the mini bundts in 2 ounces (60 g) of melted white chocolate.

NOTES

❖ Why do I call for frozen berries? Because frozen berries will stay put in the cake, while fresh berries sometimes have a tendency to float up to the top as the cake slowly bakes. Just be sure to toss them in that bit of flour before you stir them into the cake batter, to keep their juices from colouring the cake.

❖ The glaze for this recipe is not an icing that sits on top of the cake. When poured over the cake after piercing it with a few holes, the glaze soaks in just under the surface of the cake and dries, creating a sugary, slightly crisp layer over the cake. Yum—eat that part first.

Bumbleberry Tiramisu

ANGEL LOAF CAKE

6 | 6	large egg whites
1/2 tsp | 2 mL	cream of tartar
pinch | pinch	fine salt
3/4 cup | 175 mL	sugar
1 tsp | 5 mL	vanilla extract
1 tsp | 5 mL	finely grated lemon zest
1/2 cup | 125 mL	pastry flour

FILLING

5 | 5	egg yolks
1/2 cup | 125 mL	sugar
1/4 cup | 60 mL	limoncello liqueur
1 1/2 Tbsp | 22 mL	lemon juice
2 tsp | 10 mL	finely grated lemon zest
1 cup | 250 mL	whipping cream
1 Tbsp | 15 mL	vanilla extract
1 | 1	16-ounce (500-g) tub mascarpone cheese

WHIPPED CREAM

1/2 cup | 125 mL	whipping cream
2 tsp | 10 mL	sugar

LEMON SYRUP

3/4 cup | 175 mL	sugar
3/4 cup | 175 mL	water
2 tsp | 10 mL	finely grated lemon zest
1/4 cup | 60 mL	limoncello liqueur
2 Tbsp | 30 mL	fresh lemon juice

Please don't be daunted by the steps in this recipe. The cake can be made days in advance, and the assembly can be done hours ahead of your dinner guests arriving. You'll be cool as a cucumber answering the doorbell, knowing a spectacular dessert awaits, even if all else fails (and it won't—it'll be wonderful).

❖ ❖ ❖

FOR ANGEL LOAF CAKE, preheat oven to 375°F (190°C). Whip egg whites with cream of tartar and salt until they are foamy. Gradually pour in 1/2 cup (125 mL) of the sugar while whipping and continue to whip until whites hold a stiff peak (they should stand straight when beaters are lifted). Stir in vanilla. Sift pastry flour with remaining 1/4 cup (60 mL) of sugar and stir in lemon zest. Fold flour into whites gently but quickly in 3 additions. Scrape batter into an ungreased 9- × 5-inch (2-L) loaf pan and run a knife through batter to remove any large bubbles. Bake 25 to 30 minutes, until a tester inserted in the centre of the cake comes out clean. Invert pan and let cake cool completely.

FOR FILLING, whisk egg yolks with sugar, limoncello, lemon juice and zest over a pot of simmering water until doubled in volume. Remove from heat. In a separate bowl, whip cream with vanilla. Whisk mascarpone into egg mixture and fold in whipped cream. Chill until ready to assemble.

FOR WHIPPED CREAM, whip cream to soft peaks, add sugar and chill.

FOR LEMON SYRUP, heat sugar, water, and lemon zest to a simmer. Cool to room temperature and stir in limoncello and lemon juice.

ASSEMBLY

2 cups	500 mL	sliced fresh strawberries
1 cup	250 mL	fresh raspberries
1 cup	250 mL	fresh blueberries
1 cup	250 mL	fresh blackberries
		lemon zest curls, for garnish

TO ASSEMBLE, slice angel loaf into slices ½ inch (1 cm) thick and place a single layer in a large, clear trifle bowl or individual glasses. Brush cake generously with lemon syrup and spread a third of the mascarpone filling over. Toss berries and layer a third over the mascarpone. Top berries with another layer of cake and continue process two more times, finishing the tiramisu with berries. Dollop whipped cream in the centre of the tiramisu, top with just a few more berries and garnish with curls of lemon zest. Chill until ready to serve.

NOTES

✧ Who knew you could make angel food cake in a loaf pan? You still must invert the pan to cool the cake, so the cake cools to full volume (egg whites are pliable while still warm). Check out page 177 for a great trick for holding the loaf pan upside down.

✧ Limoncello is a very light Italian lemon liqueur. If not available, the same measure of sweet sherry would be lovely.

✧ Although I enjoy a traditional, coffee-laced Tiramisu, I love this summer-fresh version. It's great if you're bringing dessert to someone's house in a large glass or crystal bowl, or to make as a gift when returning a borrowed bowl (you know it's bad luck to return a borrowed plate or dish empty).

Fresh Berries

I can never get enough berries. Enjoy them now—apples and pears will be coming soon enough.

Summer Berry Pudding

SERVES 12

2 cups	500 mL	red or black currants
3 cups	750 mL	fresh raspberries
2 cups	500 mL	fresh blueberries
3 cups	750 mL	fresh blackberries
2 cups	500 mL	hulled and sliced fresh strawberries
1 1/2 cups	375 mL	sugar
3 Tbsp	45 mL	fresh lemon juice
40	40	slices white sandwich bread (about 2 loaves)

This is one of my mom's favourite desserts to make and to eat. A traditional English dessert, a bowl is lined with bread slices dipped in sweet berry juices then filled with those soft berries. Chilled and turned out, you've got summer on a plate.

✧ ✧ ✧

Combine berries, sugar and lemon juice in a heavy large saucepan. Bring just to a simmer, stirring occasionally, then remove from heat. Strain berry mixture, reserving juice and berries separately.

Line twelve 5-ounce (150-mL) ramekins with plastic wrap so it hangs over the sides. Using a 2 1/2- inch (6-cm) round cookie cutter, cut out 24 rounds from bread slices. Trim crusts from 16 remaining bread slices and cut each slice into 4 equal squares.

To build a pudding, dip 1 round slice into fruit juices and place in bottom of ramekin. Dip 5 bread squares, one at a time, into juices and place around sides of ramekin. Spoon about 1/2 cup (125 mL) berries into ramekin. Dip 1 more bread round into juices, place on top of berries and enclose with the plastic wrap hanging over the sides of the ramekin. Repeat with remaining ingredients.

Place the puddings on a baking sheet. Top with another baking sheet. Place a heavy object on baking sheet (this extracts more juices and pectins to set the puddings). Chill overnight. Combine any remaining berries and juices in bowl; cover, chill and serve with pudding if desired.

To serve, unwrap puddings. Turn out onto plates and remove plastic wrap.

[Switch Up]
Summer Berry Pudding with Berry Crème Fraîche

BERRY CRÈME FRAÎCHE

MAKES ABOUT 1 CUP (250 ML)

1 cup | 250 mL	whipping cream
1 Tbsp | 15 mL	buttermilk
1/3 cup | 75 mL	reserved berry mixture from puddings

A dollop of cream dresses up most desserts. Making use of sweet berry juices stirred into a homemade crème fraîche is even more special.

❖ ❖ ❖

FOR CRÈME FRAÎCHE, stir together cream and buttermilk, place in a glass or plastic cup or bowl and cover with plastic wrap. Immerse cup or bowl in hot water up to the level of the cream and store in a warm place (near oven or on top of fridge) for 24 to 48 hours. You'll know when it's ready because you'll see the thin-textured whey has settled at the bottom. Chill before using, being sure not to stir whey into crème fraîche (it will thin it out).

Mash reserved 1/3 cup (75 mL) berry mixture and fold into crème fraîche. Serve with Summer Berry Puddings.

NOTES

❖ It seems to defy logic, but believe me, these puddings hold their shape when unmoulded. Even made in a larger bowl, you can serve nice, even slices of this dessert.

❖ It may seem funny, but only fluffy, white sandwich bread really works for this dessert —it absorbs those fruit juices so completely.

❖ Red or black currants really help this dessert along, as they're loaded with tons of natural pectin to set the pudding. If you've missed currant season, just replace that measure with another berry, and stir 1/2 cup (125 mL) of currant jelly or jam into the berry mixture as you bring it to a simmer.

Mini Berry Tarts

CRUST

1 cup | 250 mL	unsalted butter, at room temperature
1/3 cup | 75 mL	sugar
2 | 2	large egg yolks
1 | 1	large egg
1 3/4 cup | 425 mL	all-purpose flour
1 tsp | 5 mL	fine salt

FILLING

1 cup | 250 mL	2% milk
1 | 1	vanilla bean
3 | 3	large egg yolks
3 Tbsp | 45 mL	sugar
1/4 cup | 60 mL	cornstarch
2 Tbsp | 30 mL	unsalted butter
1/2 tsp | 2 mL	almond extract
1 Tbsp | 15 mL	almond liqueur
1/4 cup | 60 mL	whipping cream

ASSEMBLY

1 cup | 250 mL	fresh raspberries
1 cup | 250 mL	fresh blueberries
1 cup | 250 mL	fresh blackberries
1/4 cup | 60 mL	sliced almonds, lightly toasted
	icing sugar, for dusting

Perfect for a casual dinner party, an elegant outdoor affair, a shower or even a wedding, these berry tarts dress up any dessert table. They're also nice passed around on a tray while everyone relaxes out on the deck after a fancy supper. Let twinkle lights abound!

◇ ◇ ◇

FOR CRUST, beat butter and sugar together until smooth. Add egg yolks and whole egg one at a time, stirring well after each addition. Stir flour and salt and blend just until dough comes together. Shape into a disk, wrap and chill for at least 2 hours before rolling.

Preheat oven to 350°F (180°C).

On a lightly floured surface, knead dough for two or three turns just to soften (this will help dough roll without cracking). Roll dough to 1/4 inch (5 mm) thick and cut out rounds to fit 24 mini tart shells. Line tart shells, prick with a fork and chill for 20 minutes. Bake for 18 to 20 minutes, until edges of shells are golden brown. Allow to cool.

FOR FILLING, heat milk with seeds scraped from pod of vanilla bean. In a bowl, whisk egg yolks, sugar and cornstarch together. Slowly pour hot milk into egg mixture while whisking, then return mixture to pot. Place over medium heat and whisk constantly until thickened and glossy, about 5 minutes. Remove from heat and strain. Stir in butter, almond extract and almond liqueur. Place plastic wrap directly on top of pastry cream and chill completely. When ready to serve, whip cream to stiff peaks and fold into chilled pastry cream.

TO ASSEMBLE, spoon or pipe a little filling into each cooled tart shell and top with a mix of berries. Arrange a few toasted almond slices on each tart and dust with icing sugar. (Tarts can be assembled up to 4 hours in advance of serving.)

NOTES

◇ I have so many recipes for sweet pastry crusts, but I find that different styles of pastry are required, depending on the filling. In this case, using a whole egg in the pastry recipe adds a crispness when you bite into it, and a little strength to hold the weight of the cream and fresh berries.

◇ When I make a pastry recipe that calls for nuts within it, I like to try and garnish with a bit of the nut, in this case the toasted almonds on top. This way, if I am not around to let people know what's in the tarts, they can see for themselves, and anyone with nut allergies is visually alerted to steer clear.

◇ Look in the grocery for disposable aluminum mini tart shells, and choose whatever size works for your occasion.

Mini Berry Tarts

My husband, Michael, and I have an expression we use when we ask each other how our day went. If we answer, "It was a golden brown day," that means it was a very good day. Why? Because everything that went into the oven comes out a perfect golden brown, even if we forgot to set the timer and just happened to pull it out of the oven in time. In other words, a golden brown day is a lucky and tasty day.

Golden brown is delectable—it is a hint of colour, a little caramelization, a bit of crunch. Nothing to excess, just perfect balance.

I wish you many golden brown days.

golden brown

PRALINE | TOFFEE | NUT BUTTERS | COOKIES | PINE NUTS
CANDY | CEREALS | CARAMELIZED SUGAR
COUNTRY SPICES | LIQUID SUGAR | GOLDEN RAISINS

Praline

Praline has two definitions in the world of desserts, and I cover both in these recipes. The European understanding of praline is sugared and caramelized nuts, usually hazelnuts or almonds. The American definition of a praline is a caramelized pecan candy. Either way, the flavour and uses are delectable and never out of fashion.

Praline Candy Dreams

MAKES ABOUT 2 DOZEN CANDIES
DESSERT SERVES 6

PRALINE CANDIES

³/₄ cup	175 mL	sugar
³/₄ cup	175 mL	light brown sugar, packed
¹/₂ cup	125 mL	whipping cream or evaporated milk
2 Tbsp	30 mL	unsalted butter
1¹/₂ cups	375 mL	pecan pieces, lightly toasted

BANANA CREAM

1 cup	250 mL	whipping cream
2 Tbsp	30 mL	sugar
1 Tbsp	15 mL	rum
2	2	bananas, sliced

NOTES

❖ Making pralines is a time-sensitive exercise. I like the method of spreading the candy into a pan to set (it takes less time). If making the New Orleans' style dropped candies, do keep the bowl in the hot water as recommended to keep the candies at an even temperature while you work with them.

❖ When served with the banana cream, the praline candies soften up just a little, just like an ice cream sundae without the brain freeze.

❖ So many shops in the French Quarter of New Orleans sold these delights. Even in the sticky heat of summer, their sweetness was still satisfying.

I spent a little time working in New Orleans and picked up this recipe along the way. The candies are firm at first bite, then yield to their pecan secret inside, melting in your mouth like creamy fudge.

❖ ❖ ❖

FOR PRALINE CANDIES, sift sugar to remove any lumps and rub brown sugar to be sure it is lump-free (this will help the candy cook evenly).

Combine both sugars, cream and butter in a heavy-bottomed saucepan and bring to a boil over medium heat. Continue boiling, brushing down the sides of the pot with water often, until it reaches 236°F (113°C). Remove from heat and let cool without stirring until 220°F (105°C), about 5 minutes. Stir praline gently with a wooden spoon for 2 minutes, until it is shiny and thickens just slightly. Stir in pecans and pour into a greased 8-inch (2-L) square pan. Another method is to drop spoonfuls of candy onto a greased parchment-lined baking sheet, but it is recommended to set pot in a bowl of hot water to maintain the temperature (the candy sets up quickly, so work fast). Break or cut into pieces to serve.

FOR BANANA CREAM, whip cream to soft peaks and stir in sugar and rum. Spoon half the cream into 6 serving dishes and top with a few slices of banana. Crumble praline candies over fruit. Top with remaining cream, banana and praline and serve immediately.

[Switch Up]
Praline Candy Dream Sundaes

HOT FUDGE SAUCE
MAKES ABOUT 1 CUP (250 ML)

²/₃ cup | 150 mL	evaporated milk
³/₄ cup | 175 mL	sugar
2 ounces | 60 g	unsweetened chocolate, chopped
2 Tbsp | 30 mL	unsalted butter
2 Tbsp | 30 mL	light corn syrup
1¹/₂ tsp | 7 mL	vanilla extract
pinch | pinch	fine salt

Serve your praline candies as part of an ice cream sundae —even after a fancy supper these are a hit.

❂ ❂ ❂

In a small heavy saucepan, heat evaporated milk and sugar over moderate heat, stirring until sugar is dissolved. Add chocolate, butter, and corn syrup to milk mixture and continue to cook, stirring constantly, just until smooth. Bring mixture to a boil over moderate heat, stirring occasionally, and gently boil 8 minutes. Remove pan from heat and stir in vanilla and salt.

To serve, scoop ice cream into serving dishes. Top with Hot Fudge Sauce and crumbled praline candies.

Fudge sauce keeps, covered and chilled, for 3 weeks. To reheat sauce, microwave uncovered on medium heat for 40 seconds, stirring occasionally.

Praline Peach Pie

CRUST

1 cup | 250 mL	whole almonds (with skins)
1 1/4 cups | 300 mL	all-purpose flour
1/2 cup | 125 mL	sugar
1/4 tsp | 1 mL	fine salt
1/2 cup | 125 mL	unsalted butter, cut into pieces and chilled
5 Tbsp | 75 mL	ice cold water

FILLING

1/2 cup | 125 mL	sugar
3 Tbsp | 45 mL	whipping cream
3 lb | 1.5 kg	fresh peaches, peeled and halved (about 10 peaches)
2 cups | 500 mL	fresh raspberries

PRALINE CRUMBLE

2/3 cup | 150 mL	sugar
2 Tbsp | 30 mL	water
1 cup | 250 mL	sliced almonds, lightly toasted
2/3 cup | 150 mL	rolled oats
1/3 cup | 75 mL	all-purpose flour
1/3 cup | 75 mL	unsalted butter, melted

NOTES

❖ The technique of reducing the peach juices in the pan with cream and sugar essentially caramelizes the fruit and concentrates their peach flavour. No soggy crusts here!

❖ The praline almonds are great to have around to top ice cream sundaes or even sprinkle, chopped, over salads.

❖ The dough for this tart is an easy, press-in style—no rolling required.

This tart is a combination of a classic peach pie and a peach crumble. The praline almonds embedded in the crumble topping add that element of surprise.

❖ ❖ ❖

FOR CRUST, pulse almonds, flour, sugar and salt in a food processor until almonds are finely ground. Add butter and pulse to a rough, crumbly texture. Add water and pulse just until dough comes together. Divide dough in half and press into a 10-inch (25-cm) tart pan. Prick pastry with a fork and chill for 30 minutes.

Preheat oven to 350°F (180°C). Bake pastry for 20 minutes, until edges are golden brown and centre is dry. Allow to cool while preparing filling.

FOR FILLING, heat sugar and whipping cream in a large sauté pan over medium high heat until bubbling. Add half of the peach halves and cook, stirring occasionally, until the liquid that cooks out of the peaches thickens and glazes peaches, about 8 minutes. Remove from heat and repeat with remaining peaches. Allow to cool. Toss with raspberries and chill until praline crumble is prepared.

FOR PRALINE CRUMBLE, cook sugar and water in a small saucepan over high heat until it caramelizes, brushing the sides of the pot often with a damp brush. Stir in toasted almonds and pour immediately onto a greased baking sheet. Allow to cool. Break praline into chunks and place in a food processor. Pulse to a rough texture. Add 1/3 cup (75 mL) of the oats, flour and melted butter and pulse until a crumbly texture. Add remaining 1/3 cup (75 mL) of oats and pulse briefly to incorporate (but not blend in completely). Spoon chilled fruit filling into pie shell and spread crumble onto fruit filling. Place on a baking sheet and bake for 30 to 40 minutes, until crumble has browned and fruit filling is bubbling.

Let pie cool to room temperature before slicing.

Toffee

A good toffee cracks at first bite, then slowly turns into a chewy, melting moment on the tip of your tongue before it almost disappears, but not without leaving a little memory of itself stuck in every space in your teeth. Beware of your dental work—this may be delicious, but it could be costly!

Caramel Toffee Squares

MAKES ONE 9-INCH (23-CM) PAN
36 SQUARES

| 6 | 6 | toffee candy bars, such as MacIntosh (about 12 ounces/360 g) |

BASE

1 1/4 cups	300 mL	all-purpose flour
1/4 cup	60 mL	sugar
1/2 tsp	2 mL	fine salt
1/2 cup	125 mL	unsalted butter, cut into pieces

TOFFEE LAYER

1/4 cup	60 mL	unsalted butter, cut into pieces
2 Tbsp	30 mL	corn syrup
2 Tbsp	30 mL	water

CHOCOLATE TOPPING

| 1 1/2 cups | 375 mL | chocolate chips |
| 3 Tbsp | 45 mL | unsalted butter, cut into pieces |

Make use of some good English toffee to add spark to these candy-like squares. Perfect for your holiday cookie tin selection.

❖ ❖ ❖

Preheat oven to 350°F (180°C) and grease a 9-inch (2.5-L) square pan. Place toffee bars in the freezer for at least one hour before making.

FOR BASE, combine flour, sugar and salt. Cut in 1/2 cup (125 mL) butter with fingers or a pastry cutter until mixture has a rough, crumbly texture and press into prepared pan. Prick base with a fork and bake 20 minutes, until edges start to brown slightly. Allow to cool.

FOR TOFFEE LAYER, remove toffee bars from freezer and place in a sealable bag. Smash bars with a rolling pin or bottom of a pot to crush into small pieces. Pour toffee pieces into a small saucepan, reserving 1/2 cup (125 mL) of pieces for the top of the squares. Add 1/4 cup (60 mL) butter, corn syrup and water and melt over medium-low heat, stirring constantly. Once smooth, pour over shortbread base and spread to coat. Bake for 10 minutes, until toffee is bubbling. Allow to cool.

FOR CHOCOLATE TOPPING, melt chocolate chips with 3 Tbsp (45 mL) butter in a bowl over a pot of gently simmering water, stirring constantly (or in microwave on medium heat, stirring at 10-second intervals, until smooth.) Spread over toffee layer and sprinkle with reserved hard toffee bits (you can smash them more if too large). Let chocolate set before slicing.

[Switch Up]
Chocolate Toffee Squares

Need a little more chocolate in your day? This Switch-Up makes for a nice visual change—try making both when building a platter or a cookie tin mix.

❖ ❖ ❖

Prepare Caramel Toffee Squares (page 128), except replace ¼ cup (60 mL) of flour with ¼ cup (60 mL) cocoa powder in the crust recipe. To finish the squares, use white chocolate instead of dark chocolate for the topping.

NOTES

❖ It is important to freeze the toffee bars so they smash to bits easily. As a kid, I used to freeze the bars before eating them. Try freezing these squares and eating them like candy from the freezer!

❖ The base for these squares is a good, basic shortbread. It will be crumbly and never really come together as a dough, but once pressed into the pan and baked, it holds its form.

❖ The difference between caramel and toffee? Caramel implies creaminess, while toffee is firmer and often chewier.

Mini Toffee Apple

Mini Toffee Apple with Maple Walnut Ice Cream

SERVES 12

12 | 12	miniature or small apples, such as MacIntosh
12 | 12	grapevine stems, chopsticks or Popsicle sticks
2 cups | 500 mL	sugar
1/2 cup | 125 mL	golden corn syrup
1/4 cup | 60 mL	water
1/2 cup | 125 mL	unsalted butter
2 tsp | 10 mL	vanilla extract
	goodies for dipping, such as chopped peanuts, chocolate chips, crisped rice cereal, etc. (optional)

These are a lovely autumn treat. I like to use the smaller apples that are often available at the farmers' market.

❖ ❖ ❖

Prepare apples by washing and drying. Stick grapevine stem, chopstick or Popsicle stick into stem end of apple and place on a parchment-lined baking tray.

Bring sugar, corn syrup and water up to a boil in a heavy-bottomed saucepan. Cook without stirring, brushing sides of the pot often with water until sugar is a light caramel colour. Remove pot from heat and whisk in butter until blended. Stir in vanilla.

While toffee is warm, dip apples, swirling and swishing to coat. If you wish, you can dip the apple bottoms in goodies to add texture. Place apples back on parchment to cool. If toffee becomes too firm for dipping, just melt over low heat, stirring gently.

Store apples in a cool dry place, but do not refrigerate. Serve with Maple Walnut Ice Cream.

NOTES

❖ Definitely get the kids involved in this task (just remember that the sugar is very hot—dip the apples for the young ones). Dunking the dipped apples in your favourite goodies makes a gooey, delicious mess (crisped rice cereal is my top pick).

❖ One warm Thanksgiving, we held a large dinner on the back deck of our cottage. I used small blackboards as placecards and toffee apples were the decoration at each place setting. My stepdaughter, Mika, 10 years old at the time, had great fun helping me.

Maple Walnut Ice Cream

MAKES ABOUT 6 CUPS (1.5 L)

1¼ cups	300 mL	2% milk
¼ cup	60 mL	maple syrup
4	4	large egg yolks
¼ cup	60 mL	sugar
1 tsp	5 mL	cornstarch
1¼ cups	300 mL	whipping cream
1 cup	250 mL	chopped walnuts, lightly toasted

NOTES

❧ The ice cream recipe only calls for a small measure of maple syrup. With nature's own toffee sauce, a little goes a long way.

This is a custard-style ice cream, made with pure maple syrup, so expect a rich custard colour, not a brown ice cream.

❖ ❖ ❖

Bring milk and maple syrup to just below a simmer in a saucepan. In a separate bowl, whisk egg yolks, sugar and cornstarch. Gradually add hot milk to egg mixture, whisking constantly until all milk has been added. Return mixture to pot and stir with a wooden spoon over medium-low heat until custard thickens and coats the back of a spoon, about 4 minutes. Remove from heat and strain. Let cool to room temperature, then stir in whipping cream. Chill custard completely.

Pour chilled custard into an ice cream maker and freeze according to manufacturer's instructions. In the last few minutes of churning, add walnuts and mix until blended. Scrape soft ice cream into a container and freeze until firm, about 4 hours.

Nut Butters

A great selection of unsweetened, pure nut butters is available not just in health food stores but on the grocery shelf as well. Often toasted, these butters can easily become a regular ingredient in your baking cupboard.

Almond Butter Cookies

MAKES ABOUT 2 DOZEN

²/₃ cup | 150 mL	unsalted butter, room temperature
¹/₂ cup | 125 mL	sugar
¹/₃ cup | 75 mL	pure almond butter
1 | 1	large egg white
¹/₄ tsp | 1 mL	vanilla extract
¹/₄ tsp | 1 mL	rum extract (optional)
1 ¹/₃ cups | 325 mL	pastry flour
¹/₄ tsp | 1 mL	fine salt
24 | 24	whole almonds

These are the "new" peanut butter cookie. Tasty and tender, they are rich in flavour, so I like to make them smaller than a standard peanut butter crisscross cookie.

❖ ❖ ❖

Preheat oven to 350°F (180°C).

Cream butter and sugar together until smooth. Beat in almond butter and egg white, then stir in vanilla extract and rum (if using). Sift in pastry flour and salt and combine until dough is soft and smooth.

Roll cookies into 1-inch (2-cm) balls and place on a parchment-lined cookie sheet an inch (2.5 cm) apart. Press a whole almond into centre of each cookie. Bake for 12 to 15 minutes on the centre rack of the oven until cookies lightly brown around the edges. Transfer cookies to a cooling rack.

NOTES

❖ Pure nut butters may behave a bit differently than major brand sweetened peanut butters, so not all peanut butter recipes are interchangeable with nut butters. You can, however, interchange nut butter flavours (almond, hazelnut, cashew, macadamia) as you wish.

❖ I love the earthy richness of toasted almond butter—Try it on a piece of whole grain toast in the morning, with a slathering of apple butter on top.

❖ Remember to store your pure nut butter in the fridge after opening. A natural separation will occur in the nut butter, and oil will rise to the top of the jar. Simply stir the butter before using again.

[Switch Up]
Chocolate Almond Butter Cookie Sandwiches

1/3 cup | 75 mL   chocolate hazelnut spread
1/4 cup | 60 mL   toasted almond butter

It's hard to decide whether these cookies are best paired with a cup of coffee or a glass of cold milk.

❖ ❖ ❖

Prepare and cool Almond Butter Cookies (page 133).

Beat chocolate hazelnut spread and almond butter until smooth. Spread on the bottom side of an almond butter cookie and sandwich filling between another cookie, pressing gently.

Cashew Butter Cupcakes

CUPCAKES

½ cup | 125 mL	cashew butter
⅓ cup | 75 mL	unsalted butter, room temperature
1½ cups | 375 mL	light brown sugar, packed
2 | 2	large eggs
1 tsp | 5 mL	vanilla extract
2 cups | 500 mL	all-purpose flour
2 tsp | 10 mL	baking powder
½ tsp | 2 mL	fine salt
¾ cup | 175 mL	2% milk, room temperature

FROSTING

¾ cup | 175 mL	whipping cream
¾ cup | 175 mL	cream cheese, room temperature
⅓ cup | 75 mL	cashew butter
3 Tbsp | 45 mL	honey
2 tsp | 10 mL	vanilla extract
	candied violets (optional)

These dainty, delicate cupcakes are great substitutes for a birthday cake, or paired with a hazelnut- or almond-flavoured coffee.

❖ ❖ ❖

FOR CUPCAKES, preheat oven to 375°F (190°C) and grease muffin tins or line with large paper cups.

Stir cashew butter before measuring to re-incorporate nut oils. Beat cashew butter and butter together until light and fluffy. Beat in brown sugar, then add eggs one at a time, mixing well after each addition. Stir in vanilla. In a separate bowl, sift flour, baking powder and salt. Add flour alternately with milk, stirring after each addition just until incorporated. Spoon batter into paper cups and bake for 20 to 25 minutes, until a tester inserted in the centre of the cupcake comes out clean. Allow to cool.

FOR FROSTING, whip cream to soft peaks and chill. Beat cream cheese until soft and fluffy, scraping down the sides of the bowl often. Beat in cashew butter and honey until smooth, and stir in vanilla. Fold in whipped cream, all in one addition, until well blended. With a small spatula or butter knife, spread generous amounts of frosting on each cupcake and top with candied violet (if using). Chill cupcakes until ready to serve (frosting will firm up somewhat).

Cupcakes should be stored in an airtight container in the fridge to prevent drying out.

NOTES

❖ The cream cheese and nut butter frosting is a great icing for a carrot cake or spice cake. Or serve it instead of butter with French toast.

❖ Try these as mini cupcakes (makes 36) for dessert "hors d'oeuvres." Just bake them for 12 to 15 minutes, and frost as usual.

Cookies

Cookies are a sweet treat themselves, but here I use them as an ingredient—double the gratification, and everyone relates to the comfort factor cookies offer. It was probably your favourite thing to bake as a kid, right?

Cookies 'n' Cream Brownies

MAKES ONE 9-INCH (2.5-L) PAN
16 BROWNIES

This recipe is a personal favourite of mine. I may not be a professed chocoholic, but when I do crave chocolate, this is my choice.

❖ ❖ ❖

FOR BROWNIES, preheat oven to 350°F (180°C). Butter and flour a 9-inch (23-cm) round cake pan, knocking out excess flour. Melt chocolate and butter in a small, heavy-bottomed saucepan over low heat, stirring until smooth. Remove from heat. Allow to cool while starting next step. In a mixing bowl, beat cream cheese until soft. Add sugar and cream until smooth. Beat in vanilla and eggs, adding one at a time and beating well after each addition. Stir in chocolate mixture. In a separate bowl sift together flour, baking powder and salt and add to chocolate mixture, beating just until batter is combined. Stir in chopped cookie chunks. Spread batter evenly in pan and bake for 25 to 30 minutes, or until a tester comes out clean. Allow brownies to cool.

FOR ICING, beat cream cheese with butter. Beat in icing sugar until smooth. Stir in vanilla and half of the cookie chunks. Spread over brownies, sprinkle with remaining cookie chunks and chill for an hour before slicing. Slice in triangles.

BROWNIES

3 1/2 ounces | 105 g	unsweetened chocolate, chopped
1/3 cup | 75 mL	unsalted butter, cut into pieces
1/2 cup | 125 mL	cream cheese, room temperature
1 cup | 250 mL	sugar
1 tsp | 5 mL	vanilla extract
2 | 2	large eggs
3/4 cup | 175 mL	all-purpose flour
1/2 tsp | 2 mL	baking powder
1/2 tsp | 2 mL	fine salt
6 | 6	chocolate sandwich cookies, chopped into chunks

ICING

1/2 cup | 125 mL	cream cheese, room temperature
1/4 cup | 60 mL	unsalted butter, room temperature
1 1/2 cups | 375 mL	icing sugar, sifted
1 1/2 tsp | 7 mL	vanilla extract
6 | 6	chocolate sandwich cookies, chopped into chunks

NOTES

❖ The cream cheese in the brownie and the icing balances the sweetness of the recipe, which is probably why this is my favourite. All I need with this is an ice-cold glass of milk.

❖ Add 1 tsp (5 mL) of any extract to the brownie to tailor the flavour—try mint, almond or orange. For a twist, use strawberry cream cheese in place of regular.

[Switch Up]
Brownie Sundae Explosion

SERVES 9

This would be a great birthday treat for someone who doesn't really want a cake, but wants to celebrate extravagantly.

❖ ❖ ❖

Prepare Hot Fudge Sauce recipe (page 126).

Slice Cookies 'n' Cream Brownies into 9 large squares and place each on a plate. Top with a generous scoop of cookies 'n' cream ice cream and slather with Hot Fudge Sauce.

Amaretti and Almond Parfait

SERVES 4

AMARETTI COOKIES

1 Tbsp | 15 mL	all-purpose flour
1 Tbsp | 15 mL	cornstarch
1 tsp | 5 mL	ground cinnamon
2/3 cup | 150 mL	sugar
1 tsp | 5 mL	finely grated lemon zest
1 cup | 250 mL	ground almonds
2 | 2	large egg whites
1 tsp | 5 mL	almond extract
1/4 cup | 60 mL	icing sugar

ALMOND CREAM

1 cup | 250 mL	mascarpone cheese
1/2 cup | 125 mL	sour cream
1/3 cup | 75 mL	light brown sugar, packed
1 tsp | 5 mL	vanilla extract
1 tsp | 5 mL	almond extract
2/3 cup | 150 mL	whipping cream

ASSEMBLY

1 1/2 cups | 375 mL	pitted sweet cherries
1 Tbsp | 15 mL	Kirsch
2 Tbsp | 30 mL	sugar
1/3 cup | 75 mL	slivered or sliced almonds, lightly toasted

Amaretti are dainty almond macaroons, traditionally served after dinner. They come wrapped in colourful papers and are a perfect accompaniment for an after-dinner espresso.

❀ ❀ ❀

FOR AMARETTI, preheat oven to 350°F (180°C) and line a baking tray with parchment paper.

Sift flour, cornstarch, cinnamon, 1/3 cup (75 mL) of the sugar and lemon zest over ground almonds and toss to blend. In a separate bowl, whip egg whites until foamy, then gradually add remaining 1/3 cup (75 mL) sugar. Whip until whites hold a stiff peak. Stir in almond mixture and add almond extract. Shape teaspoonfuls of dough into balls, wetting your hands with cool water to prevent sticking and place an inch (2.5 cm) apart on baking tray. Sift icing sugar over cookies and bake for 15 to 18 minutes, until lightly browned. Allow to cool, then store in an airtight container.

FOR ALMOND CREAM, stir mascarpone, sour cream and brown sugar together to dissolve sugar. Stir in extracts. Whip cream until soft peaks form and fold in. Chill until ready to assemble.

TO ASSEMBLE, toss cherries with Kirsch and sugar and let sit for 5 minutes.

To serve, place one amaretti cookie on a plate. Add a dollop of almond cream. Top with another amaretti cookie. Top with another dollop of almond cream, a sprinkle of toasted almonds and then a spoonful of cherries. Repeat to make 4 servings in total.

NOTES

❀ This is a sort of free-form trifle, with all the elements being assembled right before serving. Feel free to change the fruit component to whatever is tender and in season.

❀ The amaretti cookie recipe makes about 2 dozen cookies—a few extra to go with your afternoon espresso.

❀ Dusting the cookies in icing sugar creates that crackle effect as the cookie rises a little as it bakes. Like biscotti, amaretti will keep for weeks in an airtight container.

Pine Nuts

Pine nuts aren't commonly seen in desserts outside of Italy, so I think it's appropriate to embrace the Italian style of dessert, which tends to be simple and refined. The rich tenderness of pine nuts is perfect in these sweets, ideally served with a glass of Madeira after a large Italian meal.

Pine Nut Biscotti

MAKES ABOUT 2 DOZEN

1 cup + 2 Tbsp	280 mL	unsalted butter, room temperature
1 cup	250 mL	light brown sugar, packed
½ cup + 3 Tbsp	165 mL	sugar
3	3	large eggs
2 tsp	10 mL	vanilla extract
1 tsp	5 mL	almond extract
3 ⅓ cups	825 mL	all-purpose flour
⅓ cup	75 mL	durum semolina
½ tsp	2 mL	fine salt
1 ¼ cups	300 mL	lightly toasted pine nuts
¾ cup	175 mL	large bittersweet chocolate chips or chunks
		1 egg whisked with 2 Tbsp (30 mL) water, for egg wash
		turbinado sugar, for sprinkling

Everyone needs a good biscotti recipe, and the tenderness of this cookie itself matches the tenderness of the pine nuts nestled within.

❀ ❀ ❀

Preheat oven to 350° F (180°C) and line a baking sheet with parchment paper.

Cream the butter and sugars until light and fluffy. Add eggs, one at a time, until fully incorporated. Stir in extracts. In a separate bowl, sift flour, semolina and salt and add to butter mixture, stirring just until blended—dough will be soft. Stir in pine nuts and chocolate chips or chunks. Spoon mixture in 2 long rows on prepared baking sheet. With floured hands, shape evenly into 2 logs. Brush with egg wash and sprinkle with turbinado sugar. Bake for 30 minutes, until lightly browned around the edges. Allow to cool 15 minutes.

While still warm, slice biscotti into ½-inch (1-cm) slices and lay flat on baking sheet. Place baking sheet in oven and turn oven off. Biscotti will dry as oven cools, about 30 minutes.

NOTES

❀ There tend to be two styles of biscotti. The firmer style, made with all eggs and no butter, suits crunchy nuts like hazelnuts and almonds. This pine nut biscotti has a tender texture that does not require dunking in coffee to render edible.

❀ Still on the topic of tenderness, the semolina flour helps keep the biscotti tender. In place of semolina, cornmeal can be used.

❀ Dried fruit, like cranberries or figs, makes a lovely accent in place of or beside the chocolate.

[Switch Up]
Chocolate Pine Nut Biscotti

I like to mix up both chocolate and regular biscotti on a plate. Sometimes, after a very rich supper, that's all I need to serve for dessert.

❖ ❖ ❖

Replace ½ cup + ⅓ cup (200 mL) of flour in the recipe with cocoa powder, and prepare the recipe as on page 139.

Italian Pine Nut Tart (Schiacciata) with Zabaglione

CRUST

2 1/3 cups | 575 mL	all-purpose flour
1/2 cup | 125 mL	sugar
2 Tbsp | 30 mL	instant yeast
3/4 cup | 175 mL	tepid water
1 | 1	large egg yolk
pinch | pinch	fine salt

FILLING

1 lb | 450 g	black or red grapes, seeded or seedless
2/3 cup | 150 mL	lightly toasted pine nuts
1/3 cup | 75 mL	sugar

ASSEMBLY

	turbinado sugar, for sprinkling
2 Tbsp | 30 mL	extra virgin olive oil

The word schiacciata means flattened, and this recipe is a sweet Tuscan cousin to the flatbread focaccia.

❖ ❖ ❖

FOR CRUST, measure flour and sugar onto a clean work surface. Mix with your fingers and make a well in the centre. Whisk together yeast, water, egg yolk and salt and carefully pour into the centre of the flour. Using your fingers like a whisk, stir the liquid, gradually pulling in flour until a soft ball of dough forms. Dust your hands lightly with flour and knead the dough for 5 minutes. Place in an oiled bowl and cover with plastic wrap. Leave in a draft-free place until it doubles in size, about 40 minutes.

FOR FILLING, toss grapes, pine nuts and sugar and set aside.

TO ASSEMBLE, preheat oven to 350°F (180°C) and grease a 10-inch (25-cm) springform pan. Divide risen dough in half and roll one piece out 1/2 inch (1 cm) thick. Press into prepared pan and cover with half of pine nut filling. Roll out second half of dough to same size and place on top of filling, pinching the edges to seal. Top tart with remaining pine nut filling, brush with olive oil and sprinkle with turbinado sugar. Bake for 45 to 50 minutes, until top is golden brown. Serve warm or at room temperature with Zabaglione (recipe follows).

NOTES

❖ I came upon this Italian Pine Nut Tart out of necessity, working in wine country. I had a flat of Sovereign grapes (a seedless variety of Concord) and needed to use them. These grapes are available for 3 weeks in September, and if you can get your hands on some, they will make this recipe sparkle.

❖ While the base for this tart is a yeast dough, it is very user-friendly — it does not require too much kneading and is easily made by hand.

Italian Pine Nut Tart

Zabaglione

4 | 4	large egg yolks
3 Tbsp | 45 mL	sugar
¼ cup | 60 mL	Marsala wine

Whisk egg yolks and sugar in a metal bowl over a pot of gently simmering water until they turn thick and pale. Still whisking, slowly pour in Marsala, whisking until thick and creamy. Serve warm.

NOTES

❧ The zabaglione sauce keeps this dessert on the sweet side, but often I like to cut and serve this tart on a cheese board with a salty, semi-soft cheese like Taleggio or a rich cheese like Torta di Mascarpone.

Candy

Like cookies, candy can be considered not just a sweet itself, but an ingredient within desserts. Look at your favourite candy with a pastry chef's eye. There might be a new sweet treat waiting to be revealed.

Apple Toffee Turnovers

MAKES 12

1½ cups | 375 mL	peeled and grated Granny Smith apple
2 tsp | 10 mL	lemon juice
⅓ cup | 75 mL	light brown sugar, packed
1 tsp | 5 mL	ground cinnamon
1 | 1	12-ounce (360-g) package frozen puff pastry, thawed in the fridge
¾ cup | 175 mL	toffee bits
	1 egg mixed with 2 Tbsp (30 mL) water, for egg wash

This is an easy weekday treat to whip up—perfect for a packed lunch or an after-school snack.

❁ ❁ ❁

Preheat oven to 375°F (180°C) and line a baking tray with parchment paper.

Toss grated apple with lemon juice and let sit for 5 minutes. Squeeze out excess juices and toss apples with brown sugar and cinnamon.

On a lightly floured surface, roll out puff pastry into a rectangle 9 × 12 inches (21 × 30 cm). Cut dough into 3-inch (7-cm) squares, re-rolling pastry if needed. Spoon a little apple filling in centre of each square and top with toffee bits. Brush edges of pastry with egg wash and fold over to create a triangle. Pinch edges together and place on prepared baking tray. Brush tops of turnovers with remaining egg wash and bake for 20 to 25 minutes, until puffed and a rich golden brown. Serve warm or at room temperature.

NOTES

❧ Chopped walnuts or pecans, or even raisins are nice in place of toffee bits.

❧ Look for toffee bits in the baking aisle of the grocery store, alongside the chocolate chips. There are always new flavours coming out, so keep your eyes open for any hot new ideas.

Switch Up
Apple Toffee Tarts

MAKES 24 MINI TARTS

The combination of diced apple and toffee bits melted together in a tart shell may look like a butter tart, but it tastes even better.

❖ ❖ ❖

Prepare apples as above and set aside.

On a lightly floured surface, roll out pastry to 9- × 12-inch (21- × 30-cm) rectangle. Cut out circles of dough to line a 24-cup mini muffin tin or 24 mini tart shells. Re-roll pastry if needed. Prick dough with a fork. Arrange apples inside and top with toffee bits. Brush edges of pastry with egg wash. Transfer to baking sheet. Bake for 18 to 20 minutes, until puffed and a rich golden brown. Serve warm.

Almond Nougat

1 cup | 250 mL	blanched hazelnuts
1⅓ cups | 325 mL	blanched whole almonds
2 cups | 500 mL	sugar
1 cup | 250 mL	light corn syrup
½ cup | 125 mL	honey
¼ tsp | 1 mL	fine salt
¼ cup | 60 mL	water
2 | 2	large egg whites
2 tsp | 10 mL	vanilla extract
1 tsp | 5 mL	almond extract
¼ cup | 60 mL	unsalted butter, softened
½ cup | 125 mL	ground almonds

NOTES

❂ A candy thermometer is very important here to ensure you achieve a nougat with a nice texture. I also use a temperature probe thermometer—the metal thermometer is inserted in the pot and the digital display sits beside the pot and beeps when the sugar reads the right temperature.

❂ It's tempting to want to stir your sugar as it cooks, but leave it alone. Crystals will form if they spit onto the side of the pot and will grow like frost across your pot (and, sadly, there's no recovering it). Brushing the sides of the pot with water will prevent this from happening.

❂ Once set in the fridge, the nougat can be portioned into squares, wrapped in paper or plastic and put into cookie tins or wrapped for gift-giving.

This nougat recipe has an exceptional taste and texture. I use honey in the candy, which gives it an earthier colour, as opposed to a blond white.

❂ ❂ ❂

Preheat oven to 350°F (180°C). Butter an 11- × 7-inch (2-L) pan and line with parchment so that it hangs over the sides.

Place hazelnuts and whole almonds on a cookie sheet. Toast until golden, about 10 minutes.

Combine sugar, corn syrup, honey, salt and water in a heavy-bottomed saucepan. Over medium heat, stir mixture until sugar dissolves. Continue cooking without stirring until syrup reaches the hard-ball stage, reading 252°F (122°C) on a candy thermometer.

Meanwhile, in a stand mixer fitted with the whisk attachment, beat egg whites at high speed until stiff peaks form.

While mixer is on, pour ¼ cup (60 mL) of hot syrup over egg whites in a thin steady stream, beating at high speed until mixture is stiff enough to hold its shape, about 5 minutes. Continue to cook the remaining syrup to brittle threads, reading 315° to 318°F (157° to 159°C) on a candy thermometer.

While mixer is on, pour remaining hot syrup over egg whites in a thin steady stream, beating at high speed until mixture is stiff enough to hold its shape. Add vanilla extract, almond extract and butter, beating again for about 5 minutes. Stir in toasted nuts and ground almonds with a wooden spoon. Transfer mixture to the prepared pan. Smooth the mixture evenly with a spatula. If it is a particularly humid day, refrigerate until firm before slicing.

Almond Nougat

Cereals

Wholesome cereals, with built-in texture, make an excellent dessert ingredient. See…cereal's not just for breakfast anymore!

Blueberry Bran Muffins

MAKES 12 MUFFINS

2 cups | 500 mL	raisin bran cereal
3/4 cup | 175 mL	sugar
1 1/4 cups | 300 mL	all-purpose flour
1 1/4 tsp | 6 mL	baking soda
1/2 tsp | 2 mL	fine salt
1/4 cup | 60 mL	canola oil
1 | 1	large egg
1 cup | 250 mL	buttermilk
1 cup | 250 mL	fresh blueberries

This is one of the first muffin recipes I made, picked up from a little sandwich shop I worked at as a teenager. I also like these reheated the next day with a little butter.

❖ ❖ ❖

Preheat oven to 375°F (190°C) and grease a 12-cup muffin tin.

Toss cereal with sugar, flour, baking soda and salt. In a separate bowl, whisk oil, egg and buttermilk. Add buttermilk mixture to cereal mixture and stir just until blended. Stir in blueberries and spoon into prepared muffin tin. Bake for 20 to 25 minutes, until a tester inserted in the centre of a muffin comes out clean.

NOTES

❖ These muffins make great use of cereal that is just a little stale.

❖ Turn these into "hermit muffins" by adding diced apples, dates or walnuts—perfect for breakfast (just like the cereal in them).

[Switch Up]
Mini Blueberry Muffins with Lemon Cream MAKES 36 MINI MUFFINS

LEMON CREAM

MAKES ABOUT 1 1/2 CUPS (375 ML)

1/2 cup	125 mL	whipping cream, whipped to soft peaks
1/4 cup	50 mL	sour cream
1/4 cup	50 mL	sugar
2 tsp	10 mL	finely grated lemon zest
2 Tbsp	30 mL	fresh lemon juice

I like to serve these for breakfast when I have overnight guests. Any leftover lemon cream is great spooned over fresh berries.

❖ ❖ ❖

Prepare Blueberry Bran Muffins (page 148), except spoon batter into 36 greased mini muffin cups. Bake for 15 to 18 minutes, until a tester inserted in the centre of a muffin comes out clean. Serve with a dollop of lemon cream on the side.

FOR LEMON CREAM, stir whipped cream, sour cream and sugar gently together. Stir in lemon zest and juice and chill until ready to serve. Lemon cream will thicken as it sets.

Petits Fours Candies

ALMOND CRUNCHIES

2 | 2 large egg whites

½ cup	125 mL	sugar
pinch	pinch	fine salt
½ tsp	2 mL	vanilla extract
¼ tsp	1 mL	almond extract
1 cup	250 mL	corn flakes
½ cup	125 mL	chopped dates
½ cup	125 mL	slivered almonds
		icing sugar, for coating

MAKES ABOUT 1½ DOZEN

Remember bird's nests, those chocolate-covered Chinese noodle candies? Well these are as good, if not better. It's that combination of sweet, crunch and just a hint of salt that make these snackingly addictive.

❖ ❖ ❖

Preheat oven to 325°F (160°C) and line a baking tray with parchment paper.

Whip egg whites with electric mixer until foamy, then slowly add sugar and whip until whites hold a stiff peak. Fold in salt, vanilla and almond extracts, and then fold in corn flakes, dates and almonds. Drop by teaspoonfuls onto prepared tray and bake for 30 minutes. Cool completely, roll in icing sugar and store in an airtight container.

NOTES
❖ These candies are chewy, sweet AND crunchy. The dates add a flavour I really like.

PEANUT CRISPY SQUARES

½ cup	125 mL	peanut butter
½ cup	125 mL	light brown sugar, packed
½ cup	125 mL	golden corn syrup
1 cup	250 mL	chopped peanuts
4 cups	1 L	crisped rice cereal
1½ cups	375 mL	chocolate chips

MAKES ABOUT 4 DOZEN

Grease a 13- × 9-inch (3.5-L) pan and set aside.

Stir peanut butter, brown sugar and corn syrup over medium heat in a saucepan until smooth and just beginning to bubble. Stir in peanuts and cereal and press into prepared pan (dip your spatula or hand in cool water for easier spreading). Allow to cool.

Melt chocolate chips and spread over squares. Allow to set completely before cutting into squares.

NOTES
❖ Using a hot, dry knife is the easiest way to slice these treats. Just run the knife under hot tap water, wipe dry, then slice.

CHOCOLATE BANANA SLICES

3 Tbsp	45 mL	unsalted butter
5 Tbsp	75 mL	honey
2 tsp	10 mL	vanilla extract
1/2 cup	125 mL	rolled oats
1/4 cup	50 mL	dried banana chips, lightly crushed
1/4 cup	60 mL	raisins
1 Tbsp	15 mL	sweetened coconut
1 cup	250 mL	salted pretzels, lightly crushed
1 1/2 cups	375 mL	banana crunch cereal (or honey crunch cereal)
1 1/2 cups	375 mL	white chocolate chips or semi-sweet chocolate chips
1 Tbsp	15 mL	vegetable shortening

Grease an 8-inch (2-L) square pan, line with parchment paper and set aside.

Melt butter, honey and vanilla together until just beginning to bubble. Stir in oats, banana chips, raisins and coconut to coat and soften for 1 minute. Stir in pretzels and cereal until well coated and remove from heat. With lightly greased hands, press evenly into prepared pan. Let cool. Cut into 9 squares. Cut each square in half to make 2 triangles.

Stir chocolate chips with vegetable shortening in a bowl over a pot of gently simmering water until melted. Dip the candies partway in chocolate, gently shake off excess and place on baking tray to set. Drizzle tops of candies with remaining chocolate. Store in an airtight container.

NOTES

❉ This recipe makes great use of one of the fun, flavoured cereals now commonly found. Feel free to substitute a strawberry-, vanilla- or maple-flavoured cereal of a similar texture.

Caramelized Sugar

A staple in a pastry chef's kitchen, caramelized sugar is a versatile ingredient that adds taste and texture to desserts. Bless the person who first burnt their sugar by accident — we are forever grateful.

Peanut Brittle

2 cups | 500 mL	sugar
1 cup | 250 mL	golden corn syrup
1 cup | 250 mL	water
2 cups | 500 mL	unsalted peanuts
1/4 tsp | 1 mL	fine salt
1 tsp | 5 mL	unsalted butter
1 tsp | 5 mL	vanilla extract
1/4 tsp | 1 mL	baking soda

MAKES ABOUT 6 CUPS (2 L) PEANUT BRITTLE

I love the smell of cooking peanut brittle — it reminds me of autumn (just like toffee apples). I especially like it chopped into pieces and sprinkled over ice cream.

❀ ❀ ❀

Line a baking tray with parchment and grease the parchment with butter.

Combine sugar, corn syrup and water in a heavy-bottomed saucepan and bring to a boil over high heat. Without stirring, cook until it reaches the hard crack stage, about 300°F (150°C) on a candy thermometer, brushing the sides of the pot occasionally with cool water. This will take about 7 to 9 minutes, and it will turn a deep amber colour.

Remove from heat and stir in peanuts and salt with a wooden spoon. Stir in butter, vanilla and baking soda — it will immediately get foamy. Working quickly, spread nut brittle onto prepared baking sheet. Allow to set completely before cracking into pieces.

NOTES

❀ Have everything you need, such as ingredients and tools, close at hand before you begin cooking the sugar. Once you add the peanuts and the baking soda you have to work quickly, and you don't want to be running to the utensil drawer for a spoon and find the brittle hardened in the bottom of your pot.

❀ Baking soda is the secret to a tender, crackling brittle — it foams up and creates tiny bubbles within the candy, making it easier to bite into.

❀ Of course, any choice of nuts (or a blend of nuts) is up to you. I do like to lightly toast them first, before starting the brittle.

[Switch Up]
Chocolate Drizzled Peanut Brittle

If you enjoy chocolate dipped pretzels, then you'll love this combo. A little bit of *fleur de sel* sprinkled over the chocolate drizzled brittle keeps it from tasting too sweet.

❖ ❖ ❖

Prepare Peanut Brittle on page 152. Melt 4 ounces (120 g) of semisweet chocolate in a bowl over a pot of gently simmering water while stirring. Drizzle on top of brittle. Sprinkle lightly with coarse *fleur de sel* and allow chocolate to set. (*Fleur de sel* is a French sea salt available in fine food stores.)

Banana Caramel Cheesecake

Banana Caramel Cheesecake

CRUST

12 | 12	crunchy oatmeal cookies
½ cup | 125 mL	pecan pieces
¼ cup | 60 mL	unsalted butter, melted

BANANA LAYER

2 Tbsp | 30 mL	unsalted butter
¼ cup | 60 mL	light brown sugar, packed
1 tsp | 5 mL	vanilla extract
1 Tbsp | 15 mL	rum
3 | 3	firm bananas, sliced

CHEESECAKE

2 lb | 900 g	cream cheese, room temperature
1 cup | 250 mL	light brown sugar, packed
2 Tbsp | 30 mL	unsalted butter, melted
5 | 5	large eggs
2 tsp | 10 mL	vanilla extract
1 tsp | 5 mL	rum extract

Perfect wintertime decadence, but give yourself enough time to make this. Believe me — it's worth the effort.

❖ ❖ ❖

FOR CRUST, preheat oven to 350°F (180°C). Grease the bottom of a 9-inch (23-cm) springform pan and wrap the outside of the pan in foil.

In a food processor, pulse oatmeal cookies with pecans to an even crumble. Add melted butter and pulse to combine. Press into the bottom of prepared springform pan (not up the sides) and bake for 12 minutes. Allow to cool while preparing bananas.

FOR BANANA LAYER, heat a sauté pan over medium-high heat and add butter and brown sugar, stirring until melted and bubbling. Stir in vanilla and rum and add bananas. Stir just to coat and warm and pour into cooled crust.

FOR CHEESECAKE, beat cream cheese until fluffy, scraping down the sides of the bowl often. Add brown sugar in 2 additions, beating well after each addition. Beat in butter. Add eggs, one at a time, beating well after each addition. Stir in vanilla and rum extracts and pour cheesecake batter over caramelized banana layer in springform pan.

Place springform pan into a baking dish and pour hot tap water around it, to come halfway up the pan. Bake for 30 minutes, then reduce oven temperature to 325°F (160°C) and bake for another 30 to 40 minutes, until filling puffs just slightly around edges but still moves a little in centre when shaken. Remove pan from water and allow to cool for 2 hours before refrigerating overnight.

CARAMEL TOPPING

1½ cups | 375 mL   sugar

¼ cup | 60 mL   water

1 Tbsp | 15 mL   corn syrup or lemon juice

1 cup | 250 mL   whipping cream

NOTES

❂ For the crust, be sure to use crunchy oatmeal cookies without raisins, so you don't gum up your food processor.

❂ The banana layer in the cheesecake is reminiscent of that classic New Orleans dessert, Bananas Foster. Once cooked, the bananas won't turn black, but will retain that appealing caramelized appearance.

❂ When making cheesecake, beat the cream cheese and sugar on high speed as long as you like, but once you add the eggs, slow down the mixing and blend just until the eggs are incorporated—this will help prevent cracks as the cheesecake sets.

FOR CARAMEL TOPPING, combine sugar, water and corn syrup or lemon juice in a pot. Bring to a boil without stirring and cook, uncovered, until it turns a rich amber colour. While cooking, occasionally brush down the sides of the pot with a brush dipped in cool water.

Once sugar has reached desired colour, about 7 minutes, remove from heat and carefully stir in whipping cream (watch out for the steam and bubbling). Return to medium heat and simmer until reduced by a third, stirring occasionally, about 5 minutes. Chill until thickened but still fluid, about 15 minutes. Pour caramel over cheesecake and chill completely. (This can be done up to 8 hours before serving.)

To serve, run a knife carefully along the inside of the pan to loosen, remove pan and slice with a hot, dry knife.

Country Spices

Cinnamon, nutmeg, ginger, allspice and cloves... This magical combination can tempt anyone out of winter hibernation.

Spiced Country Loaf

1/2 cup | 125 mL	unsalted butter
2 Tbsp | 30 mL	fancy molasses
2 Tbsp | 30 mL	golden corn syrup
3 Tbsp | 45 mL	dark brown sugar, packed
3/4 cup | 175 mL	whole wheat flour
3/4 cup | 175 mL	all-purpose flour
1 Tbsp | 15 mL	baking powder
2 tsp | 10 mL	ground cinnamon
2 tsp | 10 mL	ground ginger
1 tsp | 5 mL	ground nutmeg
1/2 tsp | 2 mL	ground allspice
1/4 tsp | 1 mL	ground cloves
1/4 tsp | 1 mL	fine salt
2 | 2	large eggs
1/3 cup | 75 mL	2% milk, warmed
1 cup | 250 mL	applesauce
1 tsp | 5 mL	baking soda
2 Tbsp | 30 mL	ground almonds
1 cup | 250 mL	lightly toasted walnut pieces

This is a freezer staple for me. I always make a double batch and freeze one for emergency treats.

❖ ❖ ❖

Preheat oven to 350°F (180°C) and grease a 9- × 5-inch (2-L) loaf pan.

Melt butter, molasses, corn syrup and sugar until fluid and remove from heat. Stir together both flours, baking powder, spices and salt and blend into butter mixture. Stir in eggs. In a separate bowl, stir milk, apple sauce, baking soda and ground almonds and add to batter. Stir in walnuts.

Scrape batter into prepared pan and bake for 45 to 50 minutes, until a tester inserted in the centre of the cake comes out clean. Allow loaf to cool for 15 minutes, then turn out to cool completely.

NOTES

❖ I have learned never to be daunted by such a long ingredient list. This recipe is really easy to make—it's just the list of spices that makes it seem more involved.

❖ This is one of those loaves that improves the day after it's made. If you can resist the aromas of the loaf baking, it really does taste better the second day—just wrap and store on the kitchen counter (do not refrigerate).

❖ This combination of spices is sort of like a Canadian 5-spice blend. It appears in gingerbread, molasses cookies, pumpkin pie, and all things autumn.

[Switch Up]
Jumbo Muffins with Spiced Honey Glaze

SPICED HONEY GLAZE

MAKES 1/2 CUP (125 ML)

1/2 cup | 125 mL	clover honey
2 | 2	cinnamon sticks
3 | 3	whole cloves
1/4 tsp | 1 mL	ground nutmeg
2 strips | 2 strips	lemon peel
1 tsp | 5 mL	vanilla extract

The honey glaze, which is drizzled on top of these muffins, is a great topper for your favourite gingerbread recipe.

❀ ❀ ❀

Prepare Spiced Country Loaf as on page 157 and spoon batter into 6 greased jumbo muffin cups. Bake for 25 to 35 minutes, until a tester inserted in the centre of the muffin comes out clean. Serve with spiced honey glaze.

FOR SPICED HONEY GLAZE, warm all ingredients over medium-low heat for 15 minutes, then strain and drizzle over muffins. For a more intense flavour, you can leave the spices in.

Perfect Pumpkin Pie

MAKES ONE 9-INCH (23-CM) PIE
SERVES 9 TO 12

PASTRY

⅓ cup | 75 mL	unsalted butter
⅓ cup | 75 mL	vegetable shortening
1½ cups | 375 mL	all-purpose flour
2 Tbsp | 30 mL	sugar
½ tsp | 2 mL	fine salt
4 to | 60 to 5 Tbsp | 75 mL	ice water

FILLING

2 cups | 500 mL	canned pumpkin
¾ cup | 175 mL	light brown sugar, packed
3 Tbsp | 45 mL	fancy molasses
1 tsp | 5 mL	ground cinnamon
¼ tsp | 1 mL	ground nutmeg
⅛ tsp | 0.5 mL	ground cloves
½ tsp | 2 mL	fine salt
3 | 3	large eggs
1⅓ cups | 325 mL	whipping cream
3 Tbsp | 45 mL	brandy or orange liqueur

SPICED WHIPPED CREAM

1 cup | 250 mL	whipping cream
2 tsp | 10 mL	sugar
¼ tsp | 1 mL	ground cinnamon
pinch | pinch	ground nutmeg

FOR PASTRY, freeze butter and shortening for 30 minutes. Combine flour, sugar and salt in a large bowl. Using a box grater, grate the butter and shortening into flour. Toss this mixture with your fingers to coat the fats, breaking up lumps with your fingers as you go. The dough should be a rough, crumbly texture and take on a slight yellow tone. Add 4 Tbsp (60 mL) of the water and mix with a spatula or wooden spoon to bring dough together, adding a little more water if needed. Shape dough into a disk and chill for an hour before rolling.

Preheat oven to 400°F (200°C).

On a lightly floured surface, roll out dough to just under ¼ inch (5 mm) thick. Dust the bottom of a 9-inch (23-cm) pie pan with flour and line with dough. Trim edges, keeping scraps to roll and cut for garnish, if desired. Chill while preparing filling.

FOR FILLING, whisk pumpkin with brown sugar, molasses, spices and salt. Whisk in eggs, then whipping cream and brandy or orange liqueur. Pour into chilled pie shell. Bake for 10 minutes, then lower temperature to 350°F (180°C) and bake for 20 to 30 minutes, until filling puffs just a little around edges but still has a bit of jiggle in centre when moved. Allow to cool to room temperature, then chill completely.

FOR SPICED WHIPPED CREAM, whip cream with sugar and spices until medium peaks form. Dollop over the pieces of pie.

To serve pumpkin pie warm, it is recommended to bake and chill completely, then rewarm in a 300°F (150°C) oven for 15 minutes before slicing. Serve with spiced whipped cream.

NOTES

❖ The trick to a good pie crust is to get it flaky, but tender as well. The addition of a little sugar ensures tenderness, while keeping the butter and shortening cold will contribute to flakiness.

❖ A pumpkin pie filling is essentially a custard. The high heat sets the crust initially, but lowering the temperature of the oven ensures the pumpkin custard cooks gently.

❖ It is best (and easier) to make your pumpkin pie a day ahead and rewarm it rather than make it and bake it for immediate serving. If it's Thanksgiving, you no doubt have enough on your plate without worrying about the pie. By the time dessert rolls around, you should be relaxing while your family does the dishes!

Perfect Pumpkin Pie

Liquid Sugar

Honey, maple syrup, corn syrup—I'll take sugar in any form. Golden and delicious, liquid sugars add moisture and sweetness to many classic recipes.

Mini Honey Cakes

Honey adds a unique flavour to these cakes. Honey is a little fragrant and has its own special sweetness, different than regular sugar.

❖ ❖ ❖

CAKES

1 cup | 250 mL	unsalted butter, at room temperature
¼ cup | 60 mL	light brown sugar, packed
¼ cup | 60 mL	sugar
3 | 3	large eggs, at room temperature
¾ cup | 175 mL	pasteurized honey
¼ cup | 60 mL	strong coffee, room temperature
2 tsp | 10 mL	vanilla extract
2½ cups | 625 mL	pastry flour
1 tsp | 5 mL	baking powder
½ tsp | 2 mL	baking soda
½ tsp | 2 mL	fine salt
½ tsp | 2 mL	ground cinnamon
½ cup | 125 mL	raisins

GLAZE

1½ cups | 375 mL	icing sugar, sifted
2 Tbsp | 30 mL	bourbon

FOR CAKES, preheat oven to 350°F (180°C) and grease and sugar 6 mini-bundt pans, tapping out excess.

Beat butter and both sugars together until light and fluffy. Add eggs one at a time, beating well after each addition. Beat in honey, coffee and vanilla until smooth. In a separate bowl sift flour, baking powder, baking soda, salt and cinnamon. Add to butter mixture in 2 additions, stirring gently to incorporate. Stir in raisins and spoon batter into prepared pans. Bake for 35 to 40 minutes, until a tester inserted in the centre of cake comes out clean. Allow cakes to cool for 20 minutes, then turn them out to cool completely.

FOR GLAZE, stir icing sugar and bourbon together and drizzle over cakes. Let set for 30 minutes to allow glaze to firm up.

NOTES

❖ The bourbon glaze really plays off the honey nicely when drizzled over these honey cakes. If you don't wish to use bourbon, use a little cooled coffee instead.

❖ This recipe also makes a great 9- × 5- inch (2-L) loaf cake, but bake it for about 50 minutes, until a tester inserted in the centre of the loaf comes out clean.

❖ For an earthier honey taste, use buckwheat honey. If it only comes creamed at your grocery store, heat it in the microwave to melt it, let it cool, then measure.

[Switch Up]
Mini Honey Cakes with Candied Pecans and Warm Pears

WARM PEARS

3 | 3	Bartlett pears, peeled and sliced
1 Tbsp | 15 mL	unsalted butter
2 Tbsp | 30 mL	dark brown sugar
2 Tbsp | 30 mL	honey
1/2 tsp | 2 mL	ground cinnamon
1 Tbsp | 15 mL	pear brandy or lemon juice

CANDIED PECANS

1 cup | 250 mL	pecan halves
2 Tbsp | 30 mL	maple syrup
1/4 tsp | 1 mL	ground black pepper

I really like this sort of Switch-Up—it's fun to take a simple baked item and turn it into an elegant, plated dessert.

❖ ❖ ❖

Prepare Mini Honey Cakes (page 161), and serve with warm pears on the side and candied pecans sprinkled on top.

FOR WARM PEARS, melt butter in a sauté pan over medium heat and stir in sugar and honey until bubbling. Stir in sliced pears and cinnamon. Remove from heat before adding pear brandy or lemon juice, then return to heat until bubbling. Spoon onto plates to serve.

FOR CANDIED PECANS, preheat oven to 350°F (180°C) and line a baking tray with parchment.

Toss pecans with maple syrup and black pepper and spread onto baking tray. Bake for 15 minutes, stirring once halfway through. Allow to cool before using.

Frozen Maple Walnut Torte

MAPLE WALNUTS

1 1/4 cups | 300 mL	walnut pieces
1/4 cup | 60 mL	pure maple syrup

MERINGUE LAYER

4 | 4	large egg whites, room temperature
1/2 cup | 125 mL	sugar
1/2 cup | 125 mL	light brown sugar, packed

FILLING

2 1/2 cups | 625 mL	whipping cream
2/3 cup | 150 mL	pure maple syrup
1 tsp | 5 mL	vanilla extract

This is truly a favourite — I like to make it for large parties and even banquets. No ice cream maker is required — not often that you can find a frozen dessert made without one.

❈ ❈ ❈

FOR MAPLE WALNUTS, preheat oven to 350°F (180°C) and line a baking tray with parchment paper. Toss walnut pieces with maple syrup and spread on the baking tray. Toast for 12 minutes, until browned. Cool and chop finely by hand and set aside.

FOR MERINGUE, lower oven temperature to 275°F (140°C). Trace three 9-inch (23-cm) circles on a sheet of parchment paper. Place paper upside down on baking sheet.

Whip egg whites until foamy. While still whipping, pour in sugar and continue to whip until whites hold a stiff peak. Whip in brown sugar quickly (1 or 2 seconds). Spread meringue over the three circles, to 1/2 inch (1 cm) from the edge (the meringue will expand as it bakes). Bake for about an hour, until crisp (a little bit of browning is okay). Allow to cool.

FOR FILLING, whip cream to medium peaks and fold in maple syrup, vanilla and all but 3 Tbsp (45 mL) of chopped maple walnuts.

Grease and line a 9-inch (23-cm) springform pan with parchment paper. Place one meringue layer at the bottom of the pan and spread with a third of the cream. Top with second meringue layer and top with cream. Repeat with third disk and sprinkle top layer of cream with reserved 3 Tbsp (45 mL) chopped maple walnuts. Freeze overnight.

Place torte in the fridge an hour before serving, for easier slicing and to soften the meringue layers.

NOTES

❂ Try those maple walnuts on top of a salad or stirred into an autumn stuffing for chicken or pork.

❂ Brown sugar is heavier than white sugar, so be sure to fold it quickly into the whipped egg whites. It's worth the effort for that caramelized crunch.

❂ If you're making this torte right now, call me. What time can I come over?

Golden Raisins

Plump and light, golden raisins are a hit in my house over oatmeal, but they also lend sophistication to desserts. They are just a little tangier than regular Thompson raisins, so in large quantity they aren't overwhelmingly sweet.

Golden Raisin Oat Bars

MAKES ONE 9-INCH (2.5-L) SQUARE PAN
9 TO 16 SQUARES

Butter tart meets traditional square. Plump and juicy, these bars are best with a pot of Earl Grey tea.

❖ ❖ ❖

Preheat oven to 350°F (180°C) and line a 9-inch (2.5-L) square pan with parchment so it hangs over the sides.

FOR BASE, stir melted butter and both sugars together. Add flour, oats, cinnamon and salt and blend. Press mixture into prepared pan and bake for 15 minutes, until browned. Allow to cool.

FOR TOPPING, beat eggs and sugar with electric mixer until fluffy. Fold in flour, baking powder and cinnamon, then stir in raisins and coconut. Spread over cooled base and bake for 20 to 25 minutes, until golden brown. Cool before slicing.

BASE

½ cup | 125 mL	unsalted butter, melted
¼ cup | 60 mL	sugar
2 Tbsp | 30 mL	light brown sugar, packed
1 cup | 250 mL	all-purpose flour
½ cup | 125 mL	regular rolled oats (not instant)
½ tsp | 2 mL	ground cinnamon
pinch | pinch	fine salt

TOPPING

2 | 2	large eggs
1 cup | 250 mL	light brown sugar, packed
⅓ cup | 75 mL	all-purpose flour
½ tsp | 2 mL	baking powder
½ tsp | 2 mL	ground cinnamon
1⅓ cups | 325 mL	golden raisins
1 cup | 250 mL	unsweetened coconut

NOTES

❖ The most difficult part of this recipe is cooling before slicing—I love the corner piece warm, even if it's messy to slice.

❖ Beating the eggs and sugar well creates a nice crust as these bars bake. An electric mixer works best for this.

Switch Up
Oat Raisin Cobblers

2 cups | 500 mL   cranberries

2 cups | 500 mL   diced pears

²/₃ cup | 150 mL   sugar

This Switch-Up is making your dessert multi-task. The bars make for a great cobbler topping — very versatile!

❀ ❀ ❀

Prepare Golden Raisin Oat Bars (page 164).

Preheat oven to 375°F (190°C). Toss cranberries, pears and sugar. Spoon fruit mixture into 6 ramekins. Crumble about half of the Golden Raisin Oat Bars on top of fruit. Place ramekins on a baking sheet and bake 25 to 30 minutes, until fruit juices are bubbling. Serve warm.

Raisin Sugar Pie

CRUST

2 2/3 cups | 650 mL	all-purpose flour
1/3 cup | 75 mL	sugar
1/4 tsp | 1 mL	fine salt
2/3 cup | 150 mL	unsalted butter, cut into pieces and chilled
1/4 cup | 60 mL	2% milk

FILLING

1/3 cup | 75 mL	light brown sugar
1 tsp | 5 mL	ground cinnamon
1 cup | 250 mL	golden raisins
1 1/3 cups | 325 mL	whipping cream
	cinnamon, for sprinkling

Sweet and gooey, this recipe creates a caramelized cream filling, almost like Dulce de Leche (see page 42).

❖ ❖ ❖

FOR CRUST, pulse flour, sugar and salt in food processor. Add chilled butter and pulse to a rough, crumbly texture. While pulsing, add milk until dough comes together. Shape dough into a disk, wrap and chill for an hour.

Preheat oven to 425°F (220°C) and sprinkle a 9-inch (23-cm) pie plate lightly with flour. On a lightly floured surface, roll out dough to about a 10-inch (25-cm) circle and line pie plate, pinching edges.

FOR FILLING, toss sugar, cinnamon and raisins together and spread over bottom of dough. Carefully pour in cream and sprinkle top with cinnamon. Bake for 10 minutes, then reduce heat to 400°F (200°C) and bake for 30 to 35 minutes, until crust is brown and filling is browned and bubbly.

Serve pie warm or at room temperature.

NOTES

❖ This is more of a southern-style sugar pie than a Quebec-style. The cream bubbles away and caramelizes with the brown sugar. You may have to play with your oven temperature a bit. If you find it browns quickly before setting, cook a little longer at a lower temperature (no convection fan, please).

❖ I love how the golden raisins plump up in the filling as it bakes. I favour this pie over a mincemeat pie (and I really like a good mincemeat pie).

Tall, dark and handsome . . . rich brown desserts can be as enticing and intriguing as a character in a romance novel. Intense in colour and taste, these sweets will draw you in and not let you go until you have licked every crumb from your plate.

Phew . . . is it a little warm in here?

rich brown

MOLASSES | POPPY SEEDS | CAPPUCCINO | CHOCOLATE CHIPS
DOUBLE CHOCOLATE

Molasses

Molasses is a very North American ingredient. The Brits use treacle or golden syrup in their sweets, but we relish the deep, intense taste of molasses.

Gingerbread Cookies

MAKES ABOUT 2 DOZEN

½ cup | 125 mL	vegetable shortening or unsalted butter, room temperature
½ cup | 125 mL	sugar
1 | 1	large egg
1 tsp | 5 mL	vanilla extract
½ cup | 125 mL	blackstrap molasses
¼ cup | 60 mL	grated fresh ginger
3 cups | 750 mL	all-purpose flour
1 tsp | 5 mL	ground cinnamon
¾ tsp | 4 mL	baking soda
¼ tsp | 1 mL	ground cloves

This dough freezes very well, as do the baked gingerbread cookies, so get ahead on your holiday baking by making a few batches now.

❀ ❀ ❀

Cream shortening or butter and sugar until fluffy. Beat in egg and vanilla. Stir in molasses and grated ginger until evenly blended. In a separate bowl, combine remaining ingredients and add to molasses mixture, stirring just until dough comes together. Shape dough into 2 disks and chill for at least 2 hours before rolling.

Preheat oven to 375°F (190°C). On a lightly floured surface, roll out 1 disk to just over ⅛ inch (3 mm) thick. Cut out desired shapes and place on a parchment-lined baking sheet. Bake for 6 to 8 minutes, until edges are firm to touch. Allow to cool completely.

NOTES

❀ This recipe calls for blackstrap molasses, normally used in bread recipes. It has a deep, dark colour and a slightly stronger flavour. It makes for some really good-looking gingerbread men.

❀ For everyday eating I like to use butter in this recipe, but for gingerbread houses or ornaments, I use vegetable shortening.

❀ If you're using cookies as decoration, put a small hole where a string will go to tie it after cutting out your shapes.

❀ For icing (see Iced Gingerbread Cookies, page 172), play with the consistency by adding a touch more icing sugar or water. Using disposable piping bags makes for easy clean-up, and you don't even need to buy piping tips—just snip the end off the piping bag.

[Switch Up]
Iced Gingerbread Cookies

ROYAL ICING

3 Tbsp | 45 mL	meringue powder (available at cake stores and bulk stores)
1/2 cup | 125 mL	warm water
4 1/2 cups | 1.125 L	icing sugar, sifted
1 tsp | 5 mL	vanilla extract
1/2 tsp | 2 mL	cream of tartar
	paste food colours, as needed

These cookies are piped with royal icing, so you can trace outlines, smiling faces or abstract patterns. Get the whole family involved in decorating. See photo, page 32.

✧ ✧ ✧

FOR ROYAL ICING, Stir together all ingredients except colour to blend. Beat with electric mixer on high speed until mixture is stiff, about 7 minutes. Tint portions of icing as desired and keep covered with plastic wrap until ready to decorate.

Spoon icing into piping bags with plain tips, and decorate as desired.

Shoofly Pie with Gingerbread Ice Cream

This pie is the southern US version of our Canadian butter tart, but with a twist. The filling separates as it bakes, creating a cake layer that hides a soft, lusciously creamy and sweet filling underneath.

❖ ❖ ❖

CRUST

1⅓ cups | 325 mL	all-purpose flour
1 Tbsp | 15 mL	sugar
½ tsp | 2 mL	fine salt
⅔ cup | 150 mL	unsalted butter, diced and chilled
3 to | 45 to 6 Tbsp | 90 mL	ice-cold water
1 | 1	large egg white

FILLING

½ cup | 125 mL	all-purpose flour
¼ cup | 60 mL	light brown sugar, packed
¼ cup | 60 mL	unsalted butter, diced and chilled
½ cup | 125 mL	hot water
¼ tsp | 1 mL	instant coffee granules
½ tsp | 2 mL	baking soda
⅓ cup | 75 mL	golden corn syrup
3 Tbsp | 45 mL	fancy molasses
½ tsp | 2 mL	vanilla extract
pinch | pinch	fine salt
pinch | pinch	ground cinnamon

NOTES

❖ Brushing the baked pie crust with egg whites while it is still hot is a great trick. The heat of the crust sets the egg white and creates a barrier to the wet filling. A perfect technique to use on lemon squares or lemon meringue pie.

❖ Love raisins or walnuts? Stir in ½ cup (125 mL) for your own signature pie.

FOR CRUST, stir flour, sugar and salt together. Cut in cold butter until pastry is an even crumbly texture but with a few visible bits of butter. Stir in 3 Tbsp (40 mL) cold water and add remaining water a little at a time as needed, just enough to bring dough together. Shape into a disk and chill for at least one hour.

Preheat oven to 375°F (190°C). Divide dough into 6 pieces and, on a lightly floured surface, roll out each pastry piece to just less than ¼ inch (5 mm) thick. Line six 4-inch (10-cm) pie pans with pastry, tuck under rough edges and pinch or crimp to create a nice crust edge. Prick pastry with a fork. Line with aluminum foil and weight with raw rice, dried beans or pie weights. Bake for 20 minutes, remove foil and weights and bake 10 minutes more, until bottom of crust dries and becomes light golden. Remove from oven and brush lightly with egg white (this will set with the heat of the crust to create a waterproof crust). Reduce oven temperature to 350°F (180°C).

FOR FILLING, prepare while crust is baking. Combine flour and brown sugar and cut in butter to an even crumbly texture. In a separate large bowl, stir hot water and coffee granules to dissolve. Stir in baking soda, corn syrup, molasses, vanilla, salt and cinnamon into water and whisk well to combine. Spread flour crumble mixture onto baked crusts (while crusts are still hot) and pour molasses mixture over crumble—do not stir together. Bake for 35 to 40 minutes, until set (when you jiggle the tarts, they will still seem a little fluid under the crust). Let cool for at least 40 minutes before slicing.

Shoofly pie can be served warm or at room temperature. Pie can be prepared a day in advance and chilled. Serve with Gingerbread Ice Cream (recipe follows).

Gingerbread Ice Cream

1 ¼ cups | 300 mL	2% milk
⅓ cup | 75 mL	dark brown sugar, packed
2 Tbsp | 30 mL	fancy molasses
2 tsp | 10 mL	grated fresh ginger
1 tsp | 5 mL	ground cinnamon
¼ tsp | 1 mL	ground nutmeg
¼ tsp | 1 mL	ground cloves
pinch | pinch	fine salt
3 | 3	large egg yolks
1 cup | 250 mL	whipping cream

This ice cream incorporates all the lovely flavours of gingerbread cake—try it with the Perfect Pumpkin Pie (page 159) for a festive pairing.

❀ ❀ ❀

Bring milk, brown sugar, molasses, ginger, spices and salt to a simmer in a small, heavy-bottomed saucepan. In a small bowl, whisk egg yolks. Gradually add hot milk mixture to egg yolks, whisking constantly, until all milk has been incorporated. Return mixture to the pot and stir over medium-low heat until custard coats the back of a spoon, about 3 minutes. Remove from heat and strain. Chill completely.

Whisk whipping cream into custard mixture. Pour into an ice cream maker and process according to manufacturer's instructions. Scrape ice cream into a non-reactive container and keep frozen until ready to serve with Shoofly Pie.

NOTES

❀ This ice cream recipe is just too good. It's creamy and spicy, and ideal on a slice of warm apple pie or gingerbread cake.

❀ The best way to pour molasses easily from your measuring cup or spoon? Grease it before measuring the molasses.

Poppy Seeds

These little gems may get stuck in your teeth as soon as you look at them, but their light nuttiness adds spark to so many sweet goodies. My Eastern European heritage means I have inherited a love for anything with poppy seeds.

Poppy Seed Cranberry Strudel

POPPY SEED FILLING

³⁄₄ cup | 175 mL	poppy seeds
¹⁄₄ cup | 60 mL	sugar
¹⁄₃ cup | 75 mL	2% milk
1 Tbsp | 15 mL	unsalted butter
¹⁄₂ tsp | 2 mL	vanilla extract

STRUDEL

2¹⁄₂ cups | 625 mL	fresh or frozen cranberries
¹⁄₂ cup | 125 mL	sugar
¹⁄₄ cup | 60 mL	honey
1 tsp | 5 mL	vanilla extract
¹⁄₂ tsp | 2 mL	ground cinnamon
10 | 10	phyllo pastry sheets
¹⁄₄ cup | 60 mL	unsalted butter, melted
	poppy seeds for sprinkling

NOTES

❖ Grinding the poppy seeds with sugar and then cooking them in sweet milk softens them up a fair bit and extracts their delicate flavour. I use this technique if I'm making a traditional poppy seed roll for Easter.

❖ If cranberries aren't your thing (or are out of season), use apples, pears or plums.

❖ To keep phyllo from drying out while you make your strudel, cover the pastry with plastic wrap, then place a lightly dampened tea towel on the plastic wrap. The pastry will be easy to handle without getting wet.

SERVES 8

This is a snappy little dessert that is quick to put together. I love the way the phyllo pastry shatters as you crush your dessert fork into it.

❖ ❖ ❖

FOR POPPY SEED FILLING, grind poppy seeds and sugar in a food processor. Remove and scrape into a small saucepan. Stir in milk and simmer, stirring often, until milk is absorbed. Stir in butter and vanilla and set aside to cool.

FOR STRUDEL, preheat oven to 375°F (190°C). Toss cranberries with sugar, honey, vanilla and cinnamon. Spread out one sheet of phyllo pastry and brush lightly with butter. Lay another sheet of phyllo on top and brush with butter. Continue layering and brushing phyllo sheets until all are used. Spread cooled poppy seed filling along one long edge of the pastry and spoon cranberry mixture over filling. Starting with the filled side, roll up phyllo pastry to cover filling. Tuck in outside edges of pastry to seal in fruit (like folding a wrap) and continue rolling. Place strudel, seam-side down on a parchment-lined baking sheet. Brush top of strudel with butter and sprinkle with poppy seeds. Bake for 20 to 25 minutes, until pastry is a rich golden brown. Let strudel cool at least 15 minutes before slicing and serving.

Strudel is best served warm or at room temperature. It will keep chilled for up to three days.

[Switch Up]
Poppy Seed Turnovers

MAKES 10

These elegant after-dinner turnovers get rolled up just like spanakopita pockets.

❖ ❖ ❖

Simply prepare the poppy seed filling as in recipe (page 175). Spread out one sheet of phyllo pastry and brush lightly with butter. Lay another sheet of phyllo on top and brush with butter. Continue layering and brushing 3 more phyllo sheets.

Cut phyllo into 4 strips. Spoon a little cooled poppy seed filling at the end of each strip and spoon cranberries over. Fold a triangle over the fruit filling and continue folding the pastry into a triangle, sealing in the fruit. Repeat with remaining 4 sheets of phyllo.

Place turnovers, seam-side down, on a parchment-lined baking sheet. Brush tops with butter and sprinkle with poppy seeds. Bake for 18 to 20 minutes, until pastry is a rich golden brown. Serve turnovers warm or at room temperature.

Poppy Seed Cake with Lemon Ice Cream

MAKES TWO 9- × 5-INCH (2-L) LOAF PANS
SERVES 12

CAKE

6 | 6		large eggs, separated
1/2 tsp | 2 mL		cream of tartar
1 1/2 cups | 375 mL		sugar
1 1/2 cups | 375 mL		pastry flour
1/4 tsp | 1 mL		fine salt
1/2 cup | 125 mL		lemon juice
1 Tbsp | 15 mL		finely grated lemon zest
1 tsp | 5 mL		vanilla extract
3 Tbsp | 45 mL		poppy seeds

GLAZE

2 Tbsp | 30 mL		lemon juice
1 1/2 cups | 375 mL		icing sugar, sifted
1 tsp | 5 mL		finely grated lemon zest

This is a great, light-as-air, chiffon cake recipe. Paired with a creamy, rich, lemon ice cream, it's a match made in heaven.

❖ ❖ ❖

FOR CAKE, preheat oven to 325°F (160°C). Whip egg whites and cream of tartar until foamy. Gradually add 1/2 cup (125 mL) of the sugar and whip until whites hold a stiff peak. Set aside. Sift remaining 1 cup (250 mL) sugar with pastry flour and salt. In a separate bowl, whisk egg yolks, lemon juice, lemon zest and vanilla. Add yolk mixture to flour mixture and beat with electric mixer until thick and smooth, about 2 minutes. Stir in poppy seeds. Fold in a third of the whipped egg whites until almost incorporated, then fold in remaining two-thirds. Scrape batter into 2 ungreased 9- × 5-inch (2-L) loaf pans. Bake for 45 to 55 minutes (you may be tempted, but don't open the oven door for at least 35 minutes!), until a tester inserted in the centre of the cake comes out clean. Remove from oven and immediately turn the cakes upside down to cool completely. To remove cakes from pan, run a spatula or knife around the edge of the cakes and tap out onto a plate.

FOR GLAZE, stir lemon juice into icing sugar and beat until it is a thick but pourable consistency. Stir in lemon zest.

To assemble, slice cakes horizontally and spread half the glaze on the bottom layers. Replace top layers and drip remaining glaze on top. Alternatively, spread glaze over top of cakes. Serve with Lemon Ice Cream (recipe follows).

NOTES

❖ The best way to cool a cake in a loaf pan upside down? Place the loaf pan in a large bowl, so the pan sits without the cake touching the bottom.

❖ It's amazing how only 3 Tbsp (45 mL) of poppy seeds can scatter so completely throughout this cake. While delicious, it's not an ideal cake to have on a first date—you know you're going to have a poppy seed stuck right between your front teeth!

Lemon Ice Cream

MAKES ABOUT 6 CUPS (1.5 L) ICE CREAM

1/3 cup | 75 mL	fresh lemon juice
2 Tbsp | 30 mL	finely grated lemon zest
1/2 cup | 125 mL	sugar
3/4 cup | 175 mL	buttermilk
1 3/4 cups | 425 mL	whipping cream

I love lemon gelato, but this lemon ice cream is just too decadent. Tart and refreshing, yet creamy and rich, it hits such a sweet chord with me.

❖ ❖ ❖

Whisk lemon juice, zest and sugar together until sugar dissolves. Stir in buttermilk and whipping cream. Pour into ice cream maker and process according to manufacturer's instructions. Scrape ice cream into a non-reactive container and freeze until firm, about 2 hours.

Cappuccino

Some mornings I wake up thinking about coffee, and the thought of a really strong espresso topped with that frothy foamed milk is what I need to get out of bed. It's also that satisfying finish that ties together a fabulous supper.

Cappuccino Mousse

SERVES 6

2 Tbsp | 30 mL	instant coffee powder
½ cup | 125 mL	coffee, chilled
2 tsp | 10 mL	gelatin powder
2 cups | 500 mL	condensed milk
2 tsp | 10 mL	vanilla extract
2 cups | 500 mL	whipping cream
	cocoa powder or ground cinnamon, for dusting

This mousse comes together in no time and looks great in glass coffee cups or parfait glasses. The sprinkle of cocoa powder or cinnamon just caps off that cappuccino look.

❂ ❂ ❂

Stir instant coffee into chilled coffee to dissolve. Sprinkle gelatin into coffee and let soften for a minute. Stir mixture into condensed milk in a small pot. Stir over low heat until gelatin dissolves. Stir in vanilla and cool to room temperature. Whip cream to soft peaks and fold into coffee mixture in 2 additions. Spoon the mousse into serving glasses. Chill at least 2 hours.

Dust top of mousses with cocoa powder or cinnamon just before serving.

NOTES

❂ I first made this recipe for a ladies' luncheon fashion show. The theme of the show was coffee and lace (lots of frilly, tan skirts and tops), so I served this mousse garnished with a ginger lace tuile cookie.

❂ When working with gelatin, it's important to soften it first in a cold liquid so that it dissolves fully once heated. Make certain the coffee in this recipe is refrigerator cold before you begin.

❂ The condensed milk adds richness and keeps the mousse egg-free, unlike many other mousse recipes.

[Switch Up]
Mocha Latte Mousse

A layer of chocolate coffee mouse hides under the pure coffee layer, and looks fantastic served in a latte glass.

❖ ❖ ❖

Prepare Cappuccino Mousse recipe (page 179), and divide mousse in half. Stir 4 ounces (120 g) of melted semi-sweet chocolate into half of the mousse and pour into serving glasses. Top with cappuccino layer and chill. Garnish with whipped cream and a dusting of cocoa powder or cinnamon.

Cappuccino Ice Cream Cake

CRUST

16 | 16	graham crackers
1 cup | 250 mL	whole almonds
3 Tbsp | 45 mL	sugar
1/2 cup | 125 mL	unsalted butter, melted

FUDGE SAUCE

1/2 cup | 125 mL	whipping cream
1/4 cup | 60 mL	corn syrup
5 ounces | 150 g	bittersweet chocolate, chopped
1/2 tsp | 2 mL	vanilla extract
pinch | pinch	fine salt

CHOCOLATE ICE CREAM

1/2 cup | 125 mL + 3 Tbsp | + 45 mL	sugar
3 Tbsp | 45 mL	water
1 cup | 250 mL	whipping cream
1 cup | 250 mL	whole milk
6 | 6	large egg yolks
pinch | pinch	fine salt
7 ounces | 210 g	bittersweet chocolate, chopped

Sinful. The chocolate ice cream layer is so dense and deadly, just like the strong espresso layer in a cappuccino. The coffee ice cream layer that floats above it is lighter and more ephemeral, just like the foamed milk that sits on top of your coffee.

✧ ✧ ✧

FOR CRUST, preheat oven to 350°F (180°C). Pulse graham crackers, almonds and sugar until ground. Pour in melted butter and pulse until blended. Press into bottom of an ungreased 10-inch (25-cm) springform pan and bake for 12 minutes. Allow to cool.

FOR FUDGE SAUCE, heat cream and corn syrup until just below a simmer. Pour over chopped chocolate and stir until melted. Stir in vanilla and salt and set aside or chill until ready to assemble cake (reheat in microwave if necessary).

FOR CHOCOLATE ICE CREAM, bring 1/2 cup (125 mL) sugar and water to a boil in a saucepan. Without stirring, boil until sugar is a light amber colour, occasionally brushing down the sides of the pot with water. Remove from heat and carefully whisk in cream and milk (watch out for steam). If caramel hardens, return pot to low heat and stir until melted.

Whip yolks with remaining 3 Tbsp (45 mL) sugar and salt until thick and pale yellow, about 5 minutes. While whipping, slowly pour in cream mixture. Pour custard mixture into a pot and cook over medium-low heat, stirring with a wooden spoon until thickened, about 4 minutes. Strain custard over chopped chocolate and stir to melt. Chill to room temperature, then pour into cooled crust and freeze while preparing coffee ice cream.

(CONTINUES NEXT PAGE)

COFFEE ICE CREAM

2 cups | 500 mL	whipping cream
1 cup | 250 mL	whole milk
2 tsp | 10 mL	instant coffee powder
¼ cup | 60 mL	coarsely ground espresso beans
1 | 1	cinnamon stick
1 | 1	vanilla bean, split lengthwise
4 | 4	large egg yolks
10 Tbsp | 150 mL	sugar

FOR COFFEE ICE CREAM, combine 1 cup (250 mL) of the whipping cream, milk, instant coffee, espresso beans and cinnamon stick in a saucepan. Scrape seeds from vanilla bean into mixture and heat over medium-low heat. In a bowl, whisk egg yolks and sugar. While whisking, slowly pour hot cream into egg mixture. Return custard to pot and stir with a wooden spoon until thickened and custard coats the back of the spoon. Strain and chill completely. Whip remaining 1 cup (250 mL) of whipping cream to soft peaks and whisk into chilled custard. Freeze ice cream in an ice cream maker following manufacturer's instructions.

To assemble, spread all but ¼ cup (60 mL) of fudge sauce over frozen chocolate ice cream. Fudge sauce will set quickly. Spread coffee ice cream over fudge sauce and drizzle remaining sauce over coffee ice cream. Freeze for at least 4 hours before slicing.

To remove cake from pan, run a hot knife or spatula along the inside edge of the pan before removing ring.

NOTES

◈ The fudge sauce recipe is a keeper on its own—great for sundaes.

◈ I like this recipe because you make two flavours of ice cream, but you only need to use the ice cream maker once. The chocolate ice cream doesn't require any special equipment beyond an electric mixer.

◈ You'll notice that the chocolate ice cream calls for caramelizing sugar as a first step. This adds an amazing depth of flavour that works well served on its own, but is especially nice when layered against the coffee ice cream.

Chocolate Chips

When I think about baking as a child, I can picture my mom's baking cupboard, and the bag of chocolate chips that would always sit beside the baking soda and spices. Chocolate chips have to be one of the most common staples in all of our baking pantries.

Double Chocolate Chip Cookies

½ cup	125 mL	unsalted butter
8 ounces	240 g	white chocolate chips
4	4	large eggs, room temperature
1¼ cups	300 mL	sugar
2 tsp	10 mL	vanilla extract
2½ cups	625 mL	all-purpose flour
½ tsp	2 mL	baking powder
¼ tsp	1 mL	fine salt
6 ounces	180 g	semisweet chocolate chips

MAKES ABOUT 3 DOZEN

These cookies will fool you. They look just like a regular chocolate chip cookie, but in fact the cookie dough contains melted white chocolate chips.

❖ ❖ ❖

Over a pot filled with 2 inches (5 cm) of simmering water, place a metal or glass bowl and add butter. Stir until melted halfway and add white chocolate chips. Stir until just melted and remove from heat (don't worry if it separates). Set aside.

Whip eggs with sugar and vanilla until pale and thick, about 5 minutes. In a separate bowl, combine flour, baking powder and salt. Whisk melted white chocolate into egg mixture until incorporated. Whisk in flour mixture and stir in semisweet chocolate chips. Cover batter with plastic and chill for at least 4 hours before baking.

Preheat oven to 325°F (160°C). Spoon cookie dough by tablespoonfuls (or teaspoonfuls for dainty cookies) and roll gently to shape into a ball and place on a parchment-lined or greased cookie sheet, leaving 2 inches (5 cm) between cookies. Bake for 18 to 20 minutes. To test doneness, lift a cookie off the tray — if it comes off cleanly, then cookies are done. Allow to cool.

NOTES

❖ White chocolate melts at a slightly lower temperature than dark chocolate, so I melt it in a bowl over water rather than in the microwave, because I can keep an eye on it. It doesn't matter if it separates as it melts. It will come back together when mixed with everything else.

❖ This cookie batter freezes well, so it's good for emergency cookie situations, like a bad day at school, a scraped knee, or a really good movie.

[Switch Up]
Reverse Double Chocolate Chip Cookies

It's always nice to demonstrate how a recipe can have versatility, even baked goods, which have a reputation for being fixed.

✧ ✧ ✧

Prepare Double Chocolate Chip Cookies (page 183), except replace the 8 ounces (240 g) of white chocolate with 10 ounces (300 g) of bittersweet chocolate and increase sugar to 1 ½ cups (625 mL). Prepare remaining recipe as above, but stir in 6 ounces (180 g) of white chocolate chips in place of the semi-sweet chips and enjoy!

Chocolate Chip
Ice Cream Cake

CHOCOLATE CHIP COOKIE LAYERS

3/4 cup | 175 mL	unsalted butter, room temperature
1/2 cup | 125 mL	light brown sugar, packed
1/4 cup | 105 mL + 3 Tbsp |	sugar
2 Tbsp | 30 mL	golden corn syrup
1 | 1	whole large egg
1 | 1	large egg yolk
2 tsp | 10 mL	vanilla extract
1 1/2 cups | 375 mL	all-purpose flour
2 Tbsp | 30 mL	cornstarch
1 tsp | 5 mL	baking soda
1 tsp | 5 mL	fine salt
1 cup | 250 mL	miniature chocolate chips

CHOCOLATE CHIP ICE CREAM LAYER

4 | 4	large egg yolks
6 Tbsp | 90 mL	sugar
1 tsp | 5 mL	cornstarch
1 1/4 cups | 300 mL	half-and-half cream
1 tsp | 5 mL	vanilla extract
1 1/4 cups | 300 mL	whipping cream
1 1/2 cups | 375 mL	miniature chocolate chips

NOTES

❖ This cookie recipe is made especially for this ice cream cake, because it won't turn rock-solid once frozen and can be sliced relatively easily. It is important, though, to let that cake sit out for at least 15 minutes, so that the ice cream and cookie layers slice consistently.

❖ For a birthday greeting, just melt some chocolate and place it in a little piping bag to write your message.

❖ Because the top layer of this cake is a cookie, not cake, the candles won't stick in easily. To put on candles, I melt the bottom of each candle for a moment—that way the candle adheres to the cake with the melted wax and pops off easily when it's time to dig in.

I hope this becomes one of your signature birthday cakes. It's great for a birthday at any age.

❖ ❖ ❖

FOR CHOCOLATE CHIP COOKIE LAYERS, preheat oven to 325°F (160°C) and grease two 9-inch (23-cm) cake pans, lining the bottoms with parchment paper.

Cream butter, both sugars and corn syrup until smooth. Add eggs, egg yolk and vanilla and combine well. In a separate bowl, stir flour with cornstarch, baking soda and salt to blend. Add flour to butter mixture and stir until dough just comes together. Stir in chocolate chips. Divide dough evenly between the two cake pans and spread to level. Bake for 20 to 25 minutes, until cookie turns a light golden brown. Allow to cool completely.

FOR CHOCOLATE CHIP ICE CREAM, whisk egg yolks, sugar and cornstarch in a saucepan to combine. Whisk in half-and-half cream and stir mixture over medium-low heat until it thickens and become just a little glossy, about 8 minutes. Remove from heat and strain. Stir in vanilla and let mixture cool to room temperature, stirring occasionally, then chill completely. Whip cream to soft peaks and whisk into chilled cream mixture. Pour into an ice cream maker and process following the manufacturer's instructions. Just before removing ice cream, pour chocolate chips into ice cream maker and churn 30 seconds. Scrape ice cream into a container and freeze while preparing cookies for assembly (if ice cream is still quite fluid, freeze for about 40 minutes to firm up—this will prevent chocolate chips from sinking).

TO ASSEMBLE, turn cookies out of pans and peel off parchment. Line the side of a 9-inch (23-cm) springform pan with plastic wrap and place one cookie layer, top side down, into lined pan. Remove ice cream from freezer and spread over cookie. Place remaining cookie layer on top of ice cream, pressing only lightly. Wrap cake and freeze until ready to serve.

Let cake sit at room temperature for at least 15 minutes before serving. Remove springform ring and peel away plastic wrap. Slice into wedges and serve.

Double Chocolate

Is there anything better than chocolate? Yes there is — double chocolate! Dark on dark or light on dark, just give me chocolate and more of it. If there's any one request I get, it's that everyone needs more chocolate recipes. Seasonless and never out of fashion, chocolate, quite simply, makes us happy.

Marble Bundt Cake

1 cup | 250 mL	unsalted butter, room temperature
2 cups | 500 mL	sugar
4 | 4	large eggs, room temperature
2 cups | 500 mL	sour cream
2 tsp | 10 mL	vanilla extract
4 cups | 1 L	all-purpose flour
2 tsp | 10 mL	baking powder
2 tsp | 10 mL	baking soda
1 tsp | 5 mL	fine salt
4 ounces | 120 g	bittersweet chocolate, chopped and melted
3/4 cup | 175 mL	dark chocolate chips
3/4 cup | 175 mL	white chocolate chips

**MAKES ONE 12-CUP (3-L) BUNDT CAKE
SERVES 16 TO 20**

This is not your everyday bundt cake. I've upped the ante on the chocolate by stirring white chocolate chips into the dark swirls of cake and dark chocolate chips into the white swirls of cake.

❖ ❖ ❖

Preheat oven to 300°F (150°C) and grease and flour a 12-cup (3-L) bundt pan.

Beat butter and sugar together with an electric mixer until light and fluffy. Add eggs, one at a time, mixing well after each addition. Beat in sour cream and vanilla. Sift flour, baking powder, baking soda and salt and add to cake in three additions, mixing gently after each addition.

Remove 2 cups (500 mL) of batter and stir in melted bittersweet chocolate. Stir dark chocolate chips into white cake batter and stir white chocolate chips into dark batter. Dollop the different batters into prepared pan alternately, and run a knife through the cake once, swirling the batter just a little. Bake cake for 50 to 60 minutes, until a tester inserted in the centre of the cake comes out clean. Allow cake to cool for 20 minutes before turning out to cool completely.

NOTES
❖ I find a butter knife is the best "swirling" tool to use. A wooden skewer doesn't move the batter enough, and a spatula swirls too much.

❖ There's such a great selection of bundt pan styles out there, it really makes this cake present beautifully. Because of the pan shape, it's important to grease and flour the pan well, so the pan releases the cake when you tip it out.

[Switch Up]
Marble Bundt Cake with Truffle Centre

TRUFFLE CENTRE

³/₄ cup | 175 mL	whipping cream
4 ounces | 120 g	bittersweet chocolate, chopped

Adding a ganache centre really takes this crowd-pleasing cake over the top.

❊ ❊ ❊

Heat cream to just below a simmer and pour over chopped chocolate. Stir to melt and then chill until firm, about 3 hours.

To assemble, prepare Marble Bundt Cake (page 186) to the batter stage. Layer half of the 2 cake batters into prepared bundt pan, swirling as you go. Roll and shape chilled chocolate into "truffles" and lay side-by-side in a circle around the bundt pan. Top with remaining batters and bake as per recipe.

Allow cake to cool completely before slicing. You will unveil a beautiful truffle centre in each slice!

Double Chocolate Cheesecake

BROWNIE LAYER

1 cup | 250 mL	unsalted butter
1 cup | 250 mL	cocoa powder
1¾ cups | 425 mL	sugar
4 | 4	large eggs, room temperature
2 tsp | 10 mL	vanilla extract
1¼ cups | 300 mL	all-purpose flour
1 tsp | 5 mL	baking powder
½ tsp | 2 mL	fine salt
½ cup | 125 mL	white chocolate chips

CHEESECAKE LAYER

6 ounces | 180 g	semi-sweet chocolate, chopped
2 | 2	8-ounce (250-g) packages cream cheese, room temperature
½ cup | 125 mL	sugar
1 tsp | 5 mL	vanilla extract
1½ cups | 375 mL	whipping cream
2 ounces | 60 g	white chocolate, melted

Instead of a regular graham cracker crust, this cheesecake has a fudgy brownie layer beneath it.

❖ ❖ ❖

FOR BROWNIE LAYER, preheat oven to 350°F (180°C). Grease a 10-inch (25-cm) springform cake pan and line bottom and sides with parchment paper.

Melt butter and pour into a larger bowl. Sift cocoa into butter and stir in sugar. Add eggs to mixture, blending well after each addition. Stir in vanilla. In a separate bowl, combine flour, baking powder and salt (do not sift). Add to cocoa mixture and blend. Stir in white chocolate chips. Pour into pan and bake for 35 minutes, until firm. Cool completely before filling.

FOR CHEESECAKE LAYER, place chopped chocolate in a bowl over a pot of gently simmering water (be sure bowl does not touch the water) and stir to melt. Remove from heat. Beat cream cheese until fluffy with electric mixer or in a stand mixer with the whisk attachment on high speed. Slowly add sugar while mixing and beat in vanilla. Pour in whipping cream and whip on high speed, until mixture becomes firm and holds a peak. Scrape melted semi-sweet chocolate into mixture and blend quickly. Scrape filling onto brownie base and spread evenly. Chill cake for at least 2 hours before slicing.

To garnish, remove springform pan and drizzle top with white chocolate.

NOTES

❖ I prefer mixing brownie batter by hand. This ensures I don't put too much air or structure into the batter, so I end up with a dense, fudgy brownie, not a fluffy, cakey one.

❖ It doesn't matter in this recipe if you use regular or Dutch process cocoa powder. What does count is quality, though. I've always said, your chocolate desserts are only as good as the chocolate you use.

❖ The nice thing about this cheesecake is that you don't have to wait for the cheesecake to set overnight—it's a no-bake recipe that sets in about 2 hours.

Bibliography

Bailey, Lee. *Lee Bailey's Country Desserts*. New York: Gramercy Books, 1988.

Farrow, Joanna, and Sara Lewis. *Ice Cream and Iced Desserts*. London: Anness Publishing, 2000.

Greenspan, Dorie. *Baking with Julia*. New York: William Morrow and Company, 1996.

Kimball, Christopher. *The Dessert Bible*. New York: Little, Brown and Company, 2000.

Lepard, Dan, and Richard Whittington. *Baker & Spice: Baking with Passion*. London: Quadrille Publishing Limited, 1999.

The New Best Recipe. Cook's Illustrated magazine, eds. 2nd edition. Brookline: America's Test Kitchen, 2004.

Index

About the Author

✧ ✧ ✧ Anna Olson is proprietor of Olson Foods + Bakery in Port Dalhousie, Ontario, in the heart of the Niagara wine region. She and her husband, Michael, find the area a constant source of culinary inspiration, and can be regularly caught loitering at local farmers' markets.

In 2000, Anna and Michael co-authored their first book, the *Inn on the Twenty Cookbook*, followed by the 2005 release of *Anna & Michael Olson Cook at Home*, which has been shortlisted for the Cuisine Canada Cookbook of the Year 2005.

Anna has been host of the Food Network's "Sugar" for five seasons, authored the bestselling *Sugar* cookbook in 2004, and she never tires of coming up with new, decadent creations. She also shares the spotlight with co-host Jay Purvis on HGTV and the Food Network's kitchen design program, "Kitchen Equipped."

A lifetime passion for cooking became a career reality for Anna a few years after studying politics and sociology at Queen's University in Kingston, Ontario, and finally finding her way to Johnson & Wales University in Vail, Colorado, after a brief career in banking.

You'll most often find Anna puttering around her shop, sourcing out new ingredients, playing with new recipe ideas, and visiting with customers.